Kept by the
WORD

The Rise and Fall of
SATAN
and His Kingdom

Lynet Winfrey

Cover design: Brent Spears
Typesetting: Liz Smith

Printed in the United States of America

ISBN: 978-1-7346214-2-6

Dedication

Thou art worthy, O Lord, to receive glory and honour and power: for thou hast created all things, and for thy pleasure they are and were created.

Revelation 4:11

CONTENTS

INTRODUCTION

In clear detail, this book will expose the truth about Satan and his kingdom, revealing who he is, who he was, and what will become of him. It will enlighten you to his purpose for warring against God, the plans he hid in his heart, and his intentions for humanity. This book will reveal what Satan's spiritual gifts are and how he is now misusing his gifts to lure us away from the Almighty with the intent to position us to war against the Father, the Son, the Holy Spirit, the holy angels, and one another.

As you read this book, I am asking you to become teachable. Allow the Holy Spirit to inform you of spiritual matters surrounding His final work before Christ's return. It is imperative and most beneficial for every believer to have sound biblical knowledge of how the Son and the Spirit are presently moving, and of the devil's current strategies.

The Godhead and the devil are engaged in a spiritual battle that will culminate into a final cosmic war as described in Revelation 20:7–15. The battles they now are engaged in have life-or-death consequences for humanity. When a person accepts Christ, they are redeemed from Satan's captivity and kept from dying a final death in hell. But when a person chooses to continue to practice sin, they reject their only way to be saved from God's wrath against the devil, the fallen angels, and sin.

The fundamental point of salvation is that Christ died to save us from dying an eternal death. The next is that after His resurrection, He sent the Holy Spirit to convert us. Forgiveness from sin is Christ's work toward us, and conversion is the Holy Spirit's. Although forgiveness is a work Christ completed in the past, it will impart immediate effects on a person, to give the Holy Spirit a "right now" opportunity to convert that person—in the moment they confess and repent of their sin. This means the progressive nature of Christ's blood is continually present to cover a person's current sin to *always* allow that person to remain covered by His blood. This is powerful. It is the strongest testimony of the blood's strength over sin and condemnation, and the Enemy does not like this. Christ's blood strips him of every opportunity to keep an individual in a condemned state and in bondage. Please hear the Holy Spirit again. The progressive nature of Christ's blood, working through forgiveness, prevents the Enemy from keeping a person in a condemned state. A converted believer cannot be bound because Christ's blood sustains their freedom.

To spiritually grasp this, one must agree that every work Christ performs is eternal and every work the devil performs is temporary. Since this is so, Christ's blood toward us is an eternal work, a work that is continually with us from the time we were born to this present moment and even into the future. Therefore, when the Enemy deceives a believer, he must encounter the blood before he encounters that person. Why? Because a believer is covered by the eternal nature of Christ's blood and its power to sustain their salvation. In other words, due to the eternal nature of Christ's blood, if a believer commits sin, an opportunity will always be available for him to *get back up* in the moment of his sinful act or after his sinful act. This is good news! Hear the word, "A just man falls seven times and rises [gets back] up again" (Prov. 24:16). Christ's blood will always allow a person the opportunity to repent because repentance separates that person from his sin, causing him to get back up and step into right relationship with Christ.

Repentance is also what pushes back at the enemy to help keep a person out of bondage. If a person continues to live a repentant life, the fallen angels will not be able to put him or her in bondage. Fallen angels have no power over people whose lives reflect that God has forgiven them.

Therefore, due to the eternal nature of Christ's blood, know for certain His blood keeps born-again believers from being held captive by Satan. Once a person experiences true born-again conversion and remains so, he or she will not experience bondage. Satan and the fallen angels have no power over a born-again person. On the other hand, people who choose to not be converted will experience one of two types of Satanic bondage.

TWO TYPES OF BONDAGE EXPLAINED

> Woe unto them that draw iniquity with cords of vanity,
> and sin as it were with a cart rope [thick, entwined cord].
>
> – Isaiah 5:18

This text speaks of two hideous ways the Enemy tries to keep a person in bondage. The first is a bondage that comes from vanity to produce iniquity. It can simply be explained by saying the devil will entangle a person with cords of vanity. Vanity is anything harbored in the heart that can cause a person to remain in their sin. The word *iniquity* points to the type of person who is entangled. This person is a Christian, a person who knows Christ, prays, exercises spiritual gifts, yet still commits sin. Iniquity is a sinful act made only by Christians; it is Christians who practice iniquity, not unbelievers. When an unbeliever commits sin, it is called sin. When a Christian commits sin, it is called iniquity. Therefore, the word *iniquity* is reserved solely for Christians who continue to practice sin.

The best description of an iniquitous person is found in Matthew 7:22–23. In this text, a Christian approaches Christ to say, "Lord, I cast out demons in your name; prophesied in your name, and did many wonderful works in your name" to suggest to Christ that those spiritual acts validate his entrance into the kingdom. Christ's reply, "Depart from me, ye that *work iniquity*," informs how this Christian's ability to operate his spiritual gifts did not overshadow the fact that he was still committing sinful acts. That Christian thought his sins were forgiven since he could still operate his spiritual gifts. But they were not. He had one foot in the church and the other in the world. See also James 1:14–15 and 1 John 2:15–16 to gain a clear understanding of what vanity is and how a Christian can practice iniquity through their vanities.

The second type of bondage is experienced by engaging in certain sins that entangle a person with thick, entwined or twisted cords. Two kinds of this sin are described in 1 Samuel 15:23:

"Rebellion is as the sin of witchcraft." Notice the words *rebellion* and *witchcraft*. Both are acts of sin that war against God and, in turn, are actions that demonstrate how a demonic presence is living in a person to cause that person to rebel and to practice witchcraft. No human being can practice witchcraft without a fallen angel living in them. In like manner, no human being can be compelled to rebel against what is good or have a rebellious spirit without having a fallen angel living in them too. Rebellious people and participants in witchcraft, Satanism, Wicca, New Age, the dark arts, astrology, numerology, and other actions influenced by demonic activity oppose God through their craft and practices.

The phrase "draw sin with a cart rope [thick, twisted cord]" denotes how these individuals knowingly participate in demonic activity to willingly be in league with the enemy by having their soul entwined with the fallen angel's spirit that is operating in and through them. How do we know this? Pay close attention to the word *draw*. This word indicates that this individual wants to practice sin by drawing or inviting sinful activity. The words "with a cart rope" indicate how this individual has entwined, entangled, or joined himself to the fallen angel to allow that fallen angel to operate in and through him. Therefore, the bondage spoken of here is made through sins of commission—to *knowingly* do something we should not do. These acts are how a person enters into a covenant with Satan and the fallen angels, a covenant that can only be broken by the Holy Spirit.

For the sake of Christ's blood and the power of the Holy Spirit, I write this book to encourage, build up, influence, and inform every person of Satan's tactics and their right to call on holy, warring angels—angels whom the LORD has given us to keep us, holy angelic sheriffs armed and ready for battle to apprehend and overtake every foul unclean spirit that interferes with Christ's work in our lives. Family, we have been redeemed to walk boldly in the Spirit as mighty men and women who will disarm every fallen angel that gets in our way. So, suit up, and let's get to warring as one fortified spiritual body!

Decree a Thing, and It Shall Be Established unto Thee (Job 22:28)

Satan, I declare and decree that the veil of darkness and of fear has fallen! The called of God will no longer fear you and your fallen angels or those who have chosen to be in league with you! The strength of the LORD is at hand. His strength reigns in us as the sound of many roaring lions with the intent to devour your work and grind it under our feet. The called of God are moving forward in righteous indignation, to spread the gospel, compel men to become born-again, and to tear down your work that is sown in the human spirit. The Holy Spirit will rebuild the waste places of every broken human spirit that comes to Christ. He will bring every fallen angel "to ashes upon the earth . . . and never shall thou be any more" (Ezekiel 28:18–19).

Decree it, saints! Decree it!

Thou shall decree a thing, and it shall be established unto thee: and the light shall shine upon thy ways.

– Job 22:28

PART I

WHO WAS HE?

THE BEGINNING

> Thou [Lucifer] art the anointed cherub that covers.
>
> – Ezekiel 28:14

> Thou seal up the sum, full of wisdom, and perfect in beauty. . . . The workmanship of thy tabrets and of thy pipes was prepared in thee in the day thou were created.
>
> – Ezekiel 28:12–13

ORIGIN OF SATAN'S EXISTENCE

This text is rich with understanding to explain who Satan was before his fall from holiness. The phrase "in the day thou were created" is intended to show us Satan was a created being. He has a birth date, a day that points to the beginning of his existence, and he has a death date, a day that will declare the end of his life forever. His birth date and his death date are testimonies of his existence being formed by

God. Satan, therefore, was created as an angel, just as we were created to be human beings.

The word *anointed* means God sanctified him to set him apart for a specific purpose. *Cherub* is used to denote his ranking. *Covereth* illustrates his duty. The phrase "thy tabrets and...thy pipes was prepared in thee" demonstrates how he was created as a walking musical instrument. Simply speaking, God spoke an angel into existence, named him Lucifer, and bestowed on him and in him every spiritual gift he needed to live and operate as His personal, anointed, musical-covering cherub.

Thou Seal Up the Sum

The word *sum* means "the total sum of creation," everything God made. The word *seal* means the equivalent counterpart to everything God made. Therefore, the creation of Lucifer's life equaled the total sum of creation. Let's spiritually discern the matter this way:

"Thou seal up the sum"

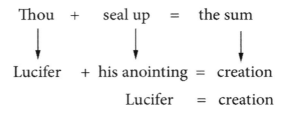

If you are not able to fully grasp the above illustration, hopefully, you will understand this point through this example. Imagine you had a two-scale balance and you placed Lucifer in one scale and everything else God created in the other scale. Noticing that the scale is now balanced, you see how Lucifer's life equaled the total sum of everything God made. The importance of this thought is to express how God's holiness, living in Lucifer, equaled the total sum of God's holiness as represented in creation. Lucifer's life was a walking representation of the collective grandeur of God's holiness, represented throughout creation.

LUCIFER'S FALL

> Thou [Lucifer] were perfect in thy ways from the day that thou were created, till iniquity was found in thee. By the multitude of thy merchandise they have filled the midst of thee with violence, and thou have sinned. ... Thine heart was lifted up because of thy beauty, thou have corrupted thy wisdom by reason of thy brightness.
>
> – Ezekiel 28:15–17

Lucifer's iniquity began when his heart was lifted up because of his beauty. What was his beauty? It was the "multitude of [his] merchandise," which is spiritually revealed to us in Ezekiel 28:12–14 as his anointing, depth of spiritual wisdom, position as the covering cherub, and the ability to be a walking musical instrument.

Since Lucifer's genetic makeup equaled the total sum of creation, and everything was created in the image of God's love, know that there was a multitude of merchandise living in Lucifer that reflected a multitude of God's love as represented in creation. Simply speaking,

9

Satan, before his fall, embodied a wealth of God's love that radiated with the grandeur of God's holiness. In other words, Lucifer's merchandise, his spiritual gifts—everything that God created in him, bestowed upon him, and imparted to him—were hallowed, blessed, and only to be used to glorify the Almighty. This merchandise is what God refers to as the beauty Satan vainly embraced to corrupt his wisdom.

Let us take a moment to understand that when Satan beheld the multitude of his merchandise through the eyes of arrogance and pride, these emotions created an unclean heart within him. This unclean heart put him in opposition to God. In the above text, this opposition is what God called violence (v. 16). Can you now see how it was in his heart that he rose up against God to oppose Him? Lucifer's unclean heart filled him with violence first before his violence was acted out to provoke the war in heaven. Family, know that war certainly originated with the devil. He used war to fight against God to oppose God's sovereignty.

As recorded in Revelation 12:7–9, the war in heaven is living proof of it being prompted and orchestrated by Satan's unclean heart. An unclean heart will always be at war with God because it is the image of Satan's heart. Please spiritually grasp the detriment of Lucifer's sin as you read Isaiah 14:12–15:

> How art thou fallen from heaven, O Lucifer, . . . for thou have said *in thine heart*, I will ascend into heaven, *I will exalt* my throne above . . . God. . . . I will be like the most High.

Lucifer, beholding the glory of the multitude of his image, corrupted his wisdom to think he resembled God and not God's image. More so than this, because love is God's image, Lucifer was created to look like love. Therefore, Lucifer sinned against God's love by thinking of himself as God and not God's image. This thought, when he meditated on it, led him to think that he, with the "merchandise" God bestowed on him and in him, could rule nations and, with these nations, overthrow God's throne to then become God. Like Esau, he "despised his birthright" (Gen. 25:34). He despised being the emblem of creation and wanted to be more. He despised being the "anointed cherub that covers" and wanted to be the Anointed One. He despised being the reflection of God's love and thereby wanted God to bear *his* image. He saw himself as being greater than God and believed he could, through his own efforts, remake himself better than how God created him. He forgot that he was created and therefore lacked power to recreate himself. Satan's action led to spiritual sin, upheaval, and blasphemy.

A person may ask why Satan desired to take God's place. Unlike some of us, Satan is well aware of the power associated with God's love. He has witnessed this power in operation, manifestation, duty, and execution. He knows this power is judicial and sovereign, and he wants to exercise its authority and enact its judiciary rights. For these reasons, Satan desires to have God's position to be in possession of His power.

The Bible reads in 1 John 4:16 that "God is love." Therefore, yield to the Holy Spirit to let Him cause your faith to honor the Father as the power of love. It was on this very point Satan went wrong. Satan thought worship was the power of love, while it is God Himself. Satan interpreted worship as the only vehicle to gain sovereign spiritual authority. We know this from Isaiah 14:13: "I will exalt my throne above God." Notice the word *exalt*. This reveals Satan's deep-seated desire to receive worship. He wanted to exalt himself to be worshiped, and he wanted to receive worship from God. It was through the act of receiving worship that Satan sought to gain sovereign authority over God.

How do we know this? Let's look at Luke 4:6–8:

> And the devil said unto him, All this power will I give thee, and the glory of them: for that is delivered unto me; and to whomsoever I will I give it. If thou therefore will worship me, all shall be thine. And Jesus answered and said unto him, Get thee behind me, Satan: for it is written, Thou shalt worship the Lord thy God, and him only shalt thou serve.

Here we read Satan saying to Christ, "All this power will I give thee . . . if thou therefore will worship me." Spiritually understand how the words "worship me" openly teach us that the only reason Satan sinned against God was to gain worship from God. He saw worship as a power tool he could use to become God. Therefore, Satan, in this verse, is tempting Christ, the one who created him, to worship him. Self-worship is the sin he hid deep in his heart. This is the sin he did not reveal to the fallen angels, and the one God exposed in Isaiah 14:12–15.

Satan Thought It Was Worship

Hear the Holy Spirit. The true nature of worship is an expression initiated by God's love living in us. When the Holy Spirit imparts His love in us, it is then that we are *made able* to worship God *through*

His love. Only God's love can produce worship, and only His love can receive worship. True worship cannot be demonstrated with the absence of God's love. That type of action is known as idolatry, which is the counterfeit of true worship. Know therefore that only God's love can produce worship to cause worship to be our spiritual response to His love. For this reason, worship is not the source of God's power, as Satan thought. The source of God's power is God Himself. Outside of God, there is no other power source. Therefore, two things are concluded here. One, Satan will never receive worship because he is incapable of imparting God's love in us to prompt us to worship him. And two, God alone is power, and all things are subject to His person.

Because the enemy is not God and is incapable of producing love, he will never receive worship. What he does receive is allegiance, not worship. The true nature of worship is spiritually reserved for God. God, therefore, has prevented worship from being duplicated. He alone is the only authentic source of love to produce worship. No one else is. The Enemy and others may think the devil is worshiped, but the true spiritual reality is he is not and can never be. What is transpiring in the Enemy's kingdom is allegiance to him and not worship. Again, since it is God's love that produces worship, worship cannot be duplicated, nor can any form of honor, allegiance, or homage be called worship. One may think those things are acts of worship. But there is only one sole form of worship, and it is what comes from God's love. Glory to your great name, Father!

SATAN'S SPIRITUAL GIFTS

Thou (Lucifer) art the anointed cherub that covers.

– Ezekiel 28:14

This sentence identifies a gift Satan uses to authenticate his supposed superiority. Each gift exercised by the fallen angels is governed by this gift, which is authority. When Satan, as Lucifer, was in heaven functioning as the anointed cherub, he exercised holy authority over all the angels. In like manner, the fallen angels are the only angels he can now exercise authority over. He has no governing authority over the remaining two-thirds holy angels.

Two examples of his authority are spiritually discerned in Job 1:6–7 and in Luke 4:5–6. In Job 1:6–7 we read, "Now there was a day when the sons of God came to present themselves before the LORD, and Satan came also among them. And the LORD said unto Satan, Whence comest thou? Then Satan answered the LORD, and said, *From going to and fro in the earth, and from walking up and down in it.*" In Luke we read, "And the devil, taking [Jesus] up into a high mountain, showed unto him all the kingdoms of the world in a moment of time. And the devil said unto him, All this power will I give thee, and the glory of them: for *that is delivered unto me; and to whomsoever I will I give it.*" The phrases "going to and fro in the earth" and "for that is delivered unto me; and to whomsoever I will I give it" denote authority—Satan's authority in the earth. Let us take a moment to understand how Satan received earthly authority.

When God created Adam, He endowed him with authority by subjecting all things under him. Genesis 1:27–28 states it this way:

14

"God created man in His own image . . . and God blessed them, and God said unto them, Be fruitful, and multiply, and replenish the earth, and subdue it: and have *dominion* over the fish of the sea, and over the fowl of the air, and over every living thing that moves upon the earth." The words "have dominion over everything that moves upon the earth" tells us Adam exercised authority over everything in the earth. When Adam sinned, he, at that moment, relinquished and transferred his earthly authority to Satan. Before Adam sinned, Satan had no legal right to exercise his authority over humanity. The only subjects Satan had authority over were the fallen angels. Satan used sin as a tool to gain authority over humans and rulership of the earth.

Though this is true, we can now glory in the fact that upon Christ's resurrection, Satan was stripped of his earthly authority. Christ says in Matthew 28:18, "All power is given unto me in heaven and in earth." Spiritually understand that through a pure and holy life, full of the Holy Ghost, mercy, and compassion, Christ strove against wickedness and gained the victory over Satan to gain all power and authority in the earth for our good. Therefore, Satan can only exercise his authority over the fallen angels and those who live in sin. But Christ exercises authority over all, both fallen angels and humanity. Alleluia!

The second spiritual gift Satan has is wisdom. Ezekiel 28:12 states that he was created as being "full of wisdom." But as you read further, verse 17 tells us that Satan has "corrupted [his] wisdom." Isaiah 14:12–14 sheds light on the corrupt nature of Satan's wisdom as what will produce sin. As soon as Satan's wisdom validated his actions to sin against God, it became corrupt. It was from this wisdom that he caused a third of the angels to doubt God, Adam and Eve to sin, and men and women to yell, "Crucify Him! Crucify Him!" at Christ's trial. Satan's wisdom is now filled with unrighteousness. His thoughts are continually evil. Christ says in John 8:44, "The devil…abode not in the truth, because there is no truth in him. When he speaks a lie, he speaks of his own: for he is a liar, and the father of it." Do you see now how Satan's wisdom is corrupt because it is full of lies? Lies are the evidence of Satan's corrupt wisdom. Therefore, the root of every lie originates from Satan's fallen wisdom. We therefore must be careful to not lie. The Word bids us to have the mind of Christ to prevent us from having the mind of fallen angels.

As such, though the Word states that Satan's wisdom is full of lies, don't be deceived to think his corrupt wisdom lacks the ability to appear uncorrupt. This is a subtle cunning action of his fallen nature. It is only by having the mind of Christ that a person will not be overtaken by Satan's fallen wisdom. Therefore, know your enemy to understand that his corrupt wisdom is what gave birth to doubt, heavenly treason, death, acts of immorality, racism, evil inventions, biological warfare, homosexuality, atheism, hatred toward God, and everything else that lacks a pure representation of righteousness.

The third spiritual gift Satan utilizes is revealed in Ezekiel 28:13. The Word says, "The workmanship of thy tabrets and of thy pipes was *prepared in thee* in the day thou were created." "Prepared in thee" indicates he was created as a walking musical instrument. The words *pipes* and *tabrets* are just an inkling of what was created in him to aid him musically to reverence God in the way of holiness that is unknown to us. He composed music that ushered in the glory of God's holiness with the most melodious form of majestic worship. From the beginning of his existence, he was created to musically celebrate God's holiness, love, and omnipotence. This was his birthright and created purpose. Thus, just as he corrupted his other gifts, so has he corrupted this gift to promote his earthly agenda.

The easiest and most accepted way for us to understand this is to agree that there are certain forms of music used in cultic and satanic circles for divinations and wicked rituals. In the same way, it is also true that many forms of secular music—rock, rap, heavy and death metal, R&B, and subtle ominous classical and contemporary instrumentals, to name a few—invite demonic activity and, sometimes, the demonic possession of a person's soul. In simple terms, the devil and the fallen angels influence the production of unrighteous music to utilize it as a tool to enter a man's soul to gain control of him. This is not only limited to lyrics but to beats also. There are unrighteous beats that invite demonic possession. There are unrighteous beats accompanied with righteous words that invite demonic possession. Even so, remember that we were created to be inhabited by the Holy Spirit and not by fallen angels. Therefore, ask God to open your ears to hear the true nature of a song so that through Christ you may believe and continue to live free from bondage by fallen angels.

Satan has three other abilities directly related to his spiritual nature that are not bound by physics, science, and time; that is, these three abilities can operate outside of our human understanding of physics, science, and time. The first two can clearly be seen and understood in Luke 4:5. Take a moment to read the verse, and we will righteously comprehend it bit by bit:

> The devil, taking [Jesus] up into a high mountain, showed
> unto him all the kingdoms of the world in a moment of
> time.

First, in the first half of the verse, "The devil, taking him up into a high mountain," you can clearly see how the devil has the ability to relocate a person from one place to another. He *took* Jesus up into a high mountain, meaning that he relocated him from one place to another.

Have no fear, though—just as this could only be performed by way of the Father allowing it, so is it the same case for us. The fallen angels cannot and will not touch us unless they receive permission from the Father. The Father will not allow the devil to touch us until He has readied us for this encounter. Believe, child, believe. Therefore, know that this performance of Satan's ability was only allowed for a specific purpose, which was to tempt Christ through a way that was familiar to Him. What do I mean? Before the Lord came to this earth as Christ, He would often transition from heaven to earth in a moment's time. In the Lord doing this, it was performed under the premise of having all power and authority. It was the All Powerful One who transitioned from heaven to earth.

Two examples include the Lord being present with the three Hebrew boys when Nebuchadnezzar commanded the men to be burned in the fiery furnace (see Dan. 3). The other account is when He visited Abraham to tell Abraham He would destroy Sodom and Gomorrah (see Gen. 18). In both cases, the Lord transitioned from heaven to earth to personally exercise His authority and execute His omnipotent judgment. The devil, knowing that Christ first exercised this ability before His incarnation, thought that by relocating Christ he would subtly appeal to Christ's divine nature as a distraction to, at the same time, entice Christ's human nature with the thought of having earthly power, which is a counterfeit for omnipotent power.

Because the Lord was now Christ the man, the devil saw Him as weak and sought to overpower Him through His human nature. Believe that the devil cunningly presented earthly power to Christ as a subtle substitute for the omnipotent power Christ first exercised as God. Christ, knowing this as well as who He is as God, rebuked Satan's attempt to lord over Him by reminding Satan that he "shall worship the Lord" his God (Luke 4:8). Christ's words were so pregnant with rebuke that the devil was immediately reminded that he was created, owns nothing, and is subject to the Creator, the very one who stood before him. It was in that moment that Satan trembled and saw the Almighty One, who birthed him into existence. Get 'em, Jesus...Get 'em!

Secondly, in the last half of our verse, "showed unto him all the kingdoms of the world in a moment of time," let us focus on the words "in a moment of time" to comprehend how angels, whether fallen or unfallen, have the ability to transition from one place to another "in a moment of time." Because the devil had to continually transition from one kingdom to the next, this very act points to the fact that the devil can only be in one place at a time. It therefore disqualifies the myth that the devil can be everywhere at the same time. This is not possible for angels. It is only possible for God. Remember, the devil is a fallen angel, not God. Nor is he a demigod. He was created as an angel and will die a fallen angel.

Thirdly, verse 6 tells us:

> And the devil said unto [Jesus], All this power will I give
> thee . . . and to whomsoever I will I give it.

> – Luke 4:6

Herein is the beginning of our understanding of the hierarchy of Satan's kingdom. Notice the words "all this power." These words demonstrate the authority Satan now exercises over certain kingdoms of the earth. A good example of this is written in Daniel 10:5–14. Please take time to read the texts below.

> Then I [Daniel] lifted up mine eyes, and looked, and
> behold a certain man clothed in linen, whose loins were
> girded with fine gold of Uphaz:

> His body also was like the beryl, and his face as the
> appearance of lightning, and his eyes as lamps of fire, and
> his arms and his feet like in colour to polished brass, and
> the voice of his words like the voice of a multitude.

> And I Daniel alone saw the vision: for the men that were
> with me saw not the vision; but a great quaking fell upon
> them, so that they fled to hide themselves.

> Therefore I was left alone, and saw this great vision, and
> there remained no strength in me: for my comeliness was
> turned in me into corruption, and I retained no strength.

> Yet heard I the voice of his words: and when I heard the
> voice of his words, then was I in a deep sleep on my face,
> and my face toward the ground.

And, behold, a hand touched me, which set me upon my knees and upon the palms of my hands.

And he said unto me, O Daniel, a man greatly beloved, understand the words that I speak unto thee, and stand upright: for unto thee am I now sent. And when he had spoken this word unto me, I stood trembling.

Then said he unto me, Fear not, Daniel: for from the first day that thou didst set thine heart to understand, and to chasten thyself before thy God, thy words were heard, and I am come for thy words.

But the prince of the kingdom of Persia withstood me one and twenty days: but, lo, Michael, one of the chief princes, came to help me; and I remained there with the kings of Persia.

Now I am come to make thee understand what shall befall thy people in the latter days: for yet the vision is for many days.

Here we read how Daniel received a vision and a holy angel clothed in linen was sent to him to give him the interpretation of that vision but was delayed by the prince of the kingdom of Persia—a fallen angel. The delayed angel (a holy angel) was confronted by the fallen angel who exercised authority over the Persian kingdom. The fallen angel tried to prevent the holy angel from reaching Daniel, but when Michael, one of the chief princes, came, the holy angel was then made able to reach Daniel. The words "in heaven" tell us that this was transpiring in the spirit realm at the same time of Daniel's fast in the earth realm.

The fallen angel over Persia is known as a territorial spirit and was appointed by Satan to rule over that kingdom. This earthly territory belonged to Satan's kingdom. But take a closer look to be aware of the purpose for this fallen angel. One, he is a prince, meaning he is in charge and has a host of fallen angels operating under him. Two, the devil appointed him to Persia to ensure that his plans were carried out. The coming of Michael, one of the chief princes, threatened the Enemy's plans because Daniel was about to receive knowledge of the rise and fall of Satan and his kingdoms.

Please note that the same Michael mentioned here is also the Michael mentioned in Revelation 12:7. He is the one who warred against the fallen angels before they were cast out of heaven. This is important to know because the chief prince Michael exhibits higher authority over that territorial spirit and the devil. Not only so, but Michael, in both instances, was the one who overpowered the devil's plans in order to execute God's plan. Do you see how the Father has mighty warring angels working on His behalf for our good? Therefore, this suggests that the chief prince Michael is the overseer of God's earthly work to see it through to its completion. Hear again the Holy Spirit—Michael will oversee God's work to its completion. Paul, in Ephesians 6:12, says, "We wrestle . . . against principalities, against powers, against the rulers of the darkness . . . against spiritual wickedness in high places," implying that we—heaven and us—are fighting against a network of Satan's kingdoms.

PART II

SATAN'S PLAN

THE DREAM

Through God's wisdom and grace, let us enter a more in-depth study of the hierarchy of Satan's kingdom as understood in Daniel 2, 5, and 8. Please read Daniel 2:1–47 below:

> And in the second year of the reign of Nebuchadnezzar, Nebuchadnezzar dreamed dreams, wherewith his spirit was troubled, and his sleep brake from him.
>
> Then the king commanded to call the magicians, and the astrologers, and the sorcerers, and the Chaldeans, for to show the king his dreams. So they came and stood before the king.
>
> And the king said unto them, I have dreamed a dream, and my spirit was troubled to know the dream.

Then spoke the Chaldeans to the king in Syriack, O king, live for ever: tell thy servants the dream, and we will show the interpretation.

The king answered and said to the Chaldeans, The thing is gone from me: if ye will not make known unto me the dream, with the interpretation thereof, ye shall be cut in pieces, and your houses shall be made a dunghill.

But if ye show the dream, and the interpretation thereof, ye shall receive of me gifts and rewards and great honour: therefore show me the dream, and the interpretation thereof.

They answered again and said, Let the king tell his servants the dream, and we will show the interpretation of it.

The king answered and said, I know of certainty that ye would gain the time, because ye see the thing is gone from me.

But if ye will not make known unto me the dream, there is but one decree for you: for ye have prepared lying and corrupt words to speak before me, till the time be changed: therefore tell me the dream, and I shall know that ye can show me the interpretation thereof.

The Chaldeans answered before the king, and said, There is not a man upon the earth that can show the king's matter: therefore there is no king, lord, nor ruler, that asked such things at any magician, or astrologer, or Chaldean.

And it is a rare thing that the king requireth, and there is none other that can show it before the king, except the gods, whose dwelling is not with flesh.

For this cause the king was angry and very furious, and commanded to destroy all the wise men of Babylon.

And the decree went forth that the wise men should be slain; and they sought Daniel and his fellows to be slain.

Then Daniel answered with counsel and wisdom to Arioch the captain of the king's guard, which was gone forth to slay the wise men of Babylon:

He answered and said to Arioch the king's captain, Why is the decree so hasty from the king? Then Arioch made the thing known to Daniel.

Then Daniel went in, and desired of the king that he would give him time, and that he would show the king the interpretation.

Then Daniel went to his house, and made the thing known to Hananiah, Mishael, and Azariah, his companions:

That they would desire mercies of the God of heaven concerning this secret; that Daniel and his fellows should not perish with the rest of the wise men of Babylon.

Then was the secret revealed unto Daniel in a night vision. Then Daniel blessed the God of heaven.

Daniel answered and said, Blessed be the name of God for ever and ever: for wisdom and might are his:

And he changeth the times and the seasons: he removeth kings, and setteth up kings: he giveth wisdom unto the wise, and knowledge to them that know understanding:

He revealeth the deep and secret things: he knoweth what is in the darkness, and the light dwelleth with him.

I thank thee, and praise thee, O thou God of my fathers, who hast given me wisdom and might, and hast made known unto me now what we desired of thee: for thou hast now made known unto us the king's matter.

Therefore Daniel went in unto Arioch, whom the king had ordained to destroy the wise men of Babylon: he went and said thus unto him; Destroy not the wise men of Babylon: bring me in before the king, and I will show unto the king the interpretation.

Then Arioch brought in Daniel before the king in haste, and said thus unto him, I have found a man of the captives of Judah, that will make known unto the king the interpretation.

The king answered and said to Daniel, whose name was Belteshazzar, Art thou able to make known unto me the dream which I have seen, and the interpretation thereof?

Daniel answered in the presence of the king, and said, The secret which the king hath demanded cannot the wise men, the astrologers, the magicians, the soothsayers, show unto the king;

But there is a God in heaven that revealeth secrets, and maketh known to the king Nebuchadnezzar what shall be in the latter days. Thy dream, and the visions of thy head upon thy bed, are these;

As for thee, O king, thy thoughts came into thy mind upon thy bed, what should come to pass hereafter: and he that revealeth secrets maketh known to thee what shall come to pass.

But as for me, this secret is not revealed to me for any wisdom that I have more than any living, but for their sakes that shall make known the interpretation to the king, and that thou mightest know the thoughts of thy heart.

Thou, O king, sawest, and behold a great image. This great image, whose brightness was excellent, stood before thee; and the form thereof was terrible.

This image's head was of fine gold, his breast and his arms of silver, his belly and his thighs of brass,

His legs of iron, his feet part of iron and part of clay.

Thou sawest till that a stone was cut out without hands, which smote the image upon his feet that were of iron and clay, and brake them to pieces.

Then was the iron, the clay, the brass, the silver, and the gold, broken to pieces together, and became like the chaff of the summer threshing floors; and the wind carried them away, that no place was found for them: and the stone that smote the image became a great mountain, and filled the whole earth.

This is the dream; and we will tell the interpretation thereof before the king.

Thou, O king, art a king of kings: for the God of heaven hath given thee a kingdom, power, and strength, and glory.

And wheresoever the children of men dwell, the beasts of the field and the fowls of the heaven hath he given into thine hand, and hath made thee ruler over them all. Thou art this head of gold.

And after thee shall arise another kingdom inferior to thee, and another third kingdom of brass, which shall bear rule over all the earth.

And the fourth kingdom shall be strong as iron: forasmuch as iron breaketh in pieces and subdueth all things: and as iron that breaketh all these, shall it break in pieces and bruise.

And whereas thou sawest the feet and toes, part of potters' clay, and part of iron, the kingdom shall be divided; but there shall be in it of the strength of the iron, forasmuch as thou sawest the iron mixed with miry clay.

And as the toes of the feet were part of iron, and part of clay, so the kingdom shall be partly strong, and partly broken.

And whereas thou sawest iron mixed with miry clay, they shall mingle themselves with the seed of men: but they shall not cleave one to another, even as iron is not mixed with clay.

And in the days of these kings shall the God of heaven set up a kingdom, which shall never be destroyed: and the kingdom shall not be left to other people, but it shall break in pieces and consume all these kingdoms, and it shall stand for ever.

Forasmuch as thou sawest that the stone was cut out of the mountain without hands, and that it brake in pieces the iron, the brass, the clay, the silver, and the gold; the great God hath made known to the king what shall come to pass hereafter: and the dream is certain, and the interpretation thereof sure.

Then the king Nebuchadnezzar fell upon his face, and worshipped Daniel, and commanded that they should offer an oblation and sweet odours unto him.

The king answered unto Daniel, and said, Of a truth it is, that your God is a God of gods, and a Lord of kings, and a revealer of secrets, seeing thou couldest reveal this secret.

Here we read about a dream Nebuchadnezzar had. He called all his astrologers, magicians, soothsayers, and Chaldeans to give him the interpretation of his dream. They could not. The first understanding Christ would have us notice is that Babylon was the seat of demonic influence and activity. How do we know? Soothsayers are mediums, present-day spirit guides, gurus, and psychics. They are people who communicate with fallen angels, which are also called demonic spirits.

A good biblical example of this is found in Acts 16:16: "As we went to prayer, a certain damsel *possessed with a spirit of divination* met us, which brought her masters much gain [money] by *soothsaying* [telling the future]." A soothsayer is a person who is willingly possessed by a fallen angel. The phrase "spirit of divination" tells us the name of the fallen angel operating through her and points out the activity this fallen angel practices through a human instrument. It also tells us the fallen angel's agenda by informing us that he divines, that is, attempts to predict the future.

Take a closer look at what is really going on, though. A spirit of divination practices actions that are a counterfeit for what the Holy Ghost does. Wow! This is dangerous because a divining fallen angel takes the seat of the Holy Ghost to tell the future. Only the Godhead has the power to speak the future into existence. And only they have the power to create what they say. No fallen angel has the power to speak a word into existence, to then create it as a thing to come to pass in the future. The best they can do is speak their agenda into your ears to have you believe in the plans they have for you in order to coax you to fall into their trap. This is not prophecy. This is a demon leading a person to accept Satan's plans for their lives. Likewise, a soothsayer is the counterfeit of a prophet. Just as the Holy Ghost uses holy men to prophesy, so do fallen angels use unholy men as psychics to speak the enemy's agenda over a person's life. Do you see the subtle trickery and sinfulness of fallen angels?

Acts 16:18 states, "Paul, being grieved, turned and said *to the spirit*, I command thee in the name of Jesus Christ to *come out* of her. And he came out the same hour." Both verses inform us that a soothsayer is a person who willingly decides to be used by a fallen angel. More importantly, the verse also shows us that the Holy Ghost and His followers have authority over fallen angels. Alleluia!

Magicians operate under the same demonic influence. An example of this is noted in Exodus 7:11 when Pharaoh called his wise men, sorcerers, and magicians, and with *enchantments* they turned a rod into a snake. The difference in how Aaron's rod turned into a snake and how the magicians' rods turned into snakes came from the source of their power. Aaron's source was God. God turned the rod into a snake. The magicians' source was enchantments, the petitioning of demonic spirits to perform this act. Don't mistake this to mean that fallen angels have creative power. This is not the case. The ability God has to speak a thing into existence, to then form it into the exact representation of His thought, lies solely with Him. No man, woman, or angel can birth God's thoughts into existence. The best that a man, woman, or fallen angel can do is replicate what God creates. This is what the enchanters did by way of demonic influence. The fallen angels took opportunity to cunningly suggest they have creative power by exercising the true nature of faith, which is to "calleth those things which be not as though they were" (Romans 4:17). This is what the fallen angels did when they turned the rod into a snake. James 2:19 tells us, "The devils also *believe*." Here we learn that the fallen angels practice faith. Their ability to turn the rod into a snake came from exercising faith.

Here are two examples. Second Kings 1:12 reads, "Elijah answered and said unto them, If I *be* a man of God, let fire come down from heaven, and consume thee and thy fifty. And the fire of God came down from heaven and consumed him and his fifty." Second, Luke 4:3 states, "And the devil said unto [Jesus], If thou be the Son of God, command this stone that it be made bread." In both instances, we understand that faith is the only vehicle by which fire came down from heaven and that the stone could turn into bread. The difference of the two is this: Christ was being tempted to exercise faith in a way that would prevent Him from relying on the Father. Had Christ turned the stone to bread, His faith would have been exercised under the pretense of sin, meaning, the faith used to turn the stone to bread would have been exercised from a sin nature and not from a holy nature. This is the same for fallen angels and enchanters. The faith used to turn their rods into snakes was exercised from a sin nature, thereby corrupting the proper use of faith.

In case you may have a hard time accepting this, let us turn our attention to Matthew 7:22–23:

> Many will say to me in that day Lord, Lord, have we not prophesied in thy name? and in thy name cast out devils? And in thy name done many wonderful works? And then will I profess unto them, I never knew you: depart from me ye that work iniquity.

The people in the above text operated their gifts by faith. But they misused their faith by operating them out of an iniquitous lifestyle. They exercised faith while at the same time living in sin. Though they cast out demons, they still practiced sin. Though they prophesied and did many wonderful things, they still willingly practiced sin. Hence, they were committing spiritual adultery against God. As such, they exercised faith from a sin nature, just like the fallen angels who turned the rods into snakes.

Understand, friend, whether a fallen angel, holy angel, or human, faith is how we respond and interact with God. In speaking about humans, just because we exercise faith to practice spiritual gifts does not necessarily mean we are born again. In fact, any person who exercises spiritual gifts and continues to willingly practice sin is practicing faith the same way fallen angels do. Therefore, do not be tricked. Love, not spiritual gifts, is the only mark of a born-again man. Hear Christ: "Every one that loveth is born of God" (1 John 4:7). Hence, everyone who loves is a man born again by God. Love alone is the mark and seal of a born-again man.

Lastly, astrologers practice enchantments through astrology. An example of God's view of astrology and those who practice it is clearly understood in Isaiah 47:9–14. In verse 13, God challenges the children of Israel to call on the astrologers and stargazers, the ones they depended on instead of Him, to save them from His judgment. He further states in verse 14 that fire shall burn them and they will not be able to save themselves. Therefore, it is scripturally concluded that Nebuchadnezzar's wise men communicated with fallen angels and practiced rituals that were of an unholy nature. This is what soothsayers, astrologers, and magicians do.

Now let us look at Nebuchadnezzar's dream to spiritually understand its interpretation as it relates to Satan building his kingdom on earth. Let us turn our attention to Daniel 2:32–33, 36, 38–40, 42:

> This image's head was of fine gold, his breast and his arms of silver, his belly and his thighs of brass,
>
> His legs of iron, his feet part of iron and part of clay....
>
> This is the dream; and we will tell the interpretation thereof before the king....
>
> Thou [King Nebuchadnezzar] art this head of gold.

And after thee shall arise another kingdom inferior to thee, and another third kingdom of brass, which shall bear rule over all the earth.

And the fourth kingdom shall be strong as iron: forasmuch as iron breaketh in pieces and subdueth all things: and as iron that breaketh all these, shall it break in pieces and bruise....

And as the toes of the feet were part of iron, and part of clay, so the kingdom shall be partly strong, and partly broken.

Daniel 2 interprets the dream as follows:

Part of statue	Represents
Head of gold	Babylon, the first kingdom
Breast and arms of brass	The second kingdom, which will overthrow Babylon
Belly and thighs of silver	The third kingdom, which will overthrow the second kingdom
Legs of iron	The fourth kingdom, which will overthrow the third kingdom
Feet of iron and clay	The fourth kingdom, which will split into ten separate kingdoms

From Daniel 2:38b and the above diagram we can spiritually conclude that Babylon is the first kingdom the enemy set up to work his evil agenda through. The other kingdoms are a succession of kingdoms Satan will use to further his plans down to the final day of judgment.

A CLEAR UNDERSTANDING OF DANIEL 2:37

> Thou, O king, art a king of kings: for the God of heaven
> hath given thee a kingdom, power, and strength, and glory.

Although God gave Babylon to Nebuchadnezzar, he ruled over it through demonic activity, rituals, and influence. To make this point simple, some think that since God gave Nebuchadnezzar Babylon, Babylon would automatically be a holy kingdom. This could only become true by way of Nebuchadnezzar's full dependence on God and not on his astrologers, soothsayers, magicians, and Chaldeans. Nebuchadnezzar's dependence on demonic activity is what corrupted the gift God gave him and is also what gave opportunity to the devil to claim this territory as his.

Here is another example. God created us, yet it is up to us to live a forgiven life. If we live a sinful life, we give opportunity to the devil to have authority over us and to claim us as his. But if we live in complete dependence on God, a born-again life is proof that we belong to Him. The demonic activity in Babylon is proof that it was under Satan's authority and was the beginning structure of his earthly kingdoms.

Take a look at Daniel 2:44–45:

> And in the days of these kings shall the God of heaven *set up a kingdom*, which shall never be destroyed: and the kingdom shall not be left to other people, but it shall break in pieces and consume all these kingdoms, and it shall stand for ever.
>
> Forasmuch as thou sawest that the stone was cut out of the mountain without hands, and that it brake in pieces the

> iron, the brass, the clay, the silver, and the gold; the great
> God hath made known to the king *what shall come to pass*
> hereafter: and the dream is certain, and the interpretation
> thereof sure.

Notice in verse 44 how God's kingdom is represented as a stone cut out of a mountain. This kingdom will break in pieces the kingdoms set up by Satan. Babylon, therefore, is the first kingdom of Satan's hierarchy of earthly kingdoms.

Two other important points are laid before us here as well. First, this verse points out how God destroys a succession of kingdoms that were in opposition to Him. Second, these kingdoms were under Satan's authority and were used by Satan to advance his methodical attack against God and us. I use the word *methodical* to illustrate how Satan is using one generation of kingdoms after another to set the stage for his present-day activity, and we can ascertain this by examining each kingdom represented by the statue. Remember, each kingdom succeeded the other by overthrowing it.

To grow in this knowledge, let's turn our attention to Daniel 7. It is another account of Nebuchadnezzar's dream but with different imagery. It records two visions, and it can be a bit confusing for first-time readers. Because of this, I have opted to use two different readings for this chapter. The first reading is copied exactly as it is written in the New King James Bible. This is for those who are familiar with Daniel 7. In the second reading, I separated both visions recorded in Daniel 7 then rearranged the verses in a specific order to give clarity and a better flow to the reading. This is for people who are not familiar with Daniel 7. If you are new to Daniel's prophecy and don't understand it, read the second reading. Don't feel intimidated by the imagery. Rather, take courage, my friend—I am certain you will understand it by the time you get to the end of this book.

First Reading:

Daniel 7 NKJV—For those who are familiar with the prophecy given to Daniel

> In the first year of Belshazzar king of Babylon, Daniel had a dream and visions of his head while on his bed. Then he wrote down the dream, telling the main facts.
>
> Daniel spoke, saying, "I saw in my vision by night, and behold, the four winds of heaven were stirring up the Great Sea. And four great beasts came up from the sea, each different from the other. The first was like a lion, and had eagle's wings. I watched till its wings were plucked off; and it was lifted up from the earth and made to stand on two feet like a man, and a man's heart was given to it.
>
> "And suddenly another beast, a second, like a bear. It was raised up on one side, and had three ribs in its mouth between its teeth. And they said thus to it: 'Arise, devour much flesh!'
>
> "After this I looked, and there was another, like a leopard, which had on its back four wings of a bird. The beast also had four heads, and dominion was given to it.
>
> "After this I saw in the night visions, and behold, a fourth beast, dreadful and terrible, exceedingly strong. It had huge iron teeth; it was devouring, breaking in pieces, and trampling the residue with its feet. It was different from all

the beasts that were before it, and it had ten horns. I was considering the horns, and there was another horn, a little one, coming up among them, before whom three of the first horns were plucked out by the roots. And there, in this horn, were eyes like the eyes of a man, and a mouth speaking pompous words.

Vision of the Ancient of Days

"I watched till thrones were put in place,
And the Ancient of Days was seated;
His garment *was* white as snow,
And the hair of His head was like pure wool.
His throne was a fiery flame,
Its wheels a burning fire;
A fiery stream issued and came forth from before Him.
A thousand thousands ministered to Him;
Ten thousand times ten thousand stood before Him.
The court was seated, and the books were opened.

"I watched then because of the sound of the pompous words which the horn was speaking; I watched till the beast was slain, and its body destroyed and given to the burning flame. As for the rest of the beasts, they had their dominion taken away, yet their lives were prolonged for a season and a time.

"I was watching in the night visions, and behold,
One like the Son of Man,
Coming with the clouds of heaven!
He came to the Ancient of Days,
And they brought Him near before Him.

Then to Him was given dominion and glory
  and a kingdom,
That all peoples, nations, and languages should
  serve Him.
His dominion is an everlasting dominion,
Which shall not pass away,
And His kingdom the one
Which shall not be destroyed.

Daniel's Visions Interpreted

"I, Daniel, was grieved in my spirit within my body, and the visions of my head troubled me. I came near to one of those who stood by, and asked him the truth of all this. So he told me and made known to me the interpretation of these things: 'Those great beasts, which are four, are four kings which arise out of the earth. But the saints of the Most High shall receive the kingdom, and possess the kingdom forever, even forever and ever.'

"Then I wished to know the truth about the fourth beast, which was different from all the others, exceedingly dreadful, with its teeth of iron and its nails of bronze, which devoured, broke in pieces, and trampled the residue with its feet; and the ten horns that were on its head, and the other horn which came up, before which three fell, namely, that horn which had eyes and a mouth which spoke pompous words, whose appearance was greater than his fellows.

"I was watching; and the same horn was making war against the saints, and prevailing against them, until the

Ancient of Days came, and a judgment was made in favor of the saints of the Most High, and the time came for the saints to possess the kingdom.

"Thus he said:

> 'The fourth beast shall be
> a fourth kingdom on earth,
> which shall be different from all *other* kingdoms,
> and shall devour the whole earth,
> trample it and break it in pieces.
> The ten horns are ten kings
> Who shall arise from this kingdom.
> And another shall rise after them;
> He shall be different from the first ones,
> And shall subdue three kings.
> He shall speak pompous words against the Most High,
> Shall persecute the saints of the Most High,
> And shall intend to change times and law.
> Then *the saints* shall be given into his hand
> For a time and times and half a time.
> 'But the court shall be seated,
> And they shall take away his dominion,
> To consume and destroy *it* forever.
> Then the kingdom and dominion,
> And the greatness of the kingdoms under the whole heaven,
> Shall be given to the people, the saints of the Most High.
> His kingdom *is* an everlasting kingdom,
> And all dominions shall serve and obey Him.'

"This *is* the end of the account. As for me, Daniel, my thoughts greatly troubled me, and my countenance changed; but I kept the matter in my heart."

Second Reading:

Daniel 7 Rearranged—For those who are new to this prophecy that was given to Daniel

Second Vision—Daniel 7:13, 10a, 9b2, 9b1, 9a, and 10b

13 "I was watching in the night visions, And behold, One like the Son of Man [Jesus],

Coming with the clouds [angels] of heaven! He came to the Ancient of Days [God the Father], And they [the angels] brought Him [Christ] near before Him [the Father].

10a A fiery stream issued and came forth from before Him [Christ]: [a] thousand thousands ministered to Him, and ten thousand times ten thousand stood before Him.

9b2 His garment was white as snow, And the hair of His head was like pure wool. His throne was a fiery flame, its wheels a burning fire;

9b1 And the Ancient of Days [the Father] was seated;

9a "I watched till thrones were put in place,

10b The court was seated, and the books were opened.

The phrases "the court was seated" and "the books were opened" are key to understanding what's going on in these verses. To do this, we must also read

Revelation 20:11a, 12b, 12a1, 11b, 13, 14a and 15 in this order:

[11a] Then I saw a great white throne and Him who sat on it...

[12b] and the books were opened.

STOP!

Can you see that the throne mentioned here and the open books inform us that both accounts are of the same event? Therefore, read carefully, as Revelation will tell us exactly what event Daniel saw. Let's start from the beginning again.

[11a] Then I saw a great white throne and Him who sat on it...

[12b] and the books were opened. And another book was opened, which is the Book of Life.

[12a1] And I saw the dead, small and great, standing before God, from whose face the earth and the heaven fled away. And there was found no place for them.

[11b] And the dead were judged according to their works, by the things which were written in the books.

[13] The sea gave up the dead who were in it, and Death and Hades [hell] delivered up the dead who were in them. And they were judged, each one according to his works.

[14] Then Death and Hades [hell] were cast into the lake of fire...

[15] And anyone not found written in the Book of Life was cast into the lake of fire.

Both visions are of the final judgment day when a court will convene in heaven. At that time, Christ will have finished interceding for us. He then will take off His priestly robe and put on His kingly robe to present Himself to the Ancient of Days (the Father) and to sit down on His throne as God and not as the Son of God. There is a difference. He in that moment will be equal with the Father and the Holy Spirit and will function in that capacity throughout eternity. Right now, He is functioning as the Son of God, as our intercessor. But when judgment day comes, He will transition from being the Son of God to being I AM, who He was before His incarnation. When this happens, I AM will open the books, and all who did not accept the salvation that came from His incarnate life will experience the wrath of the Father, the Spirit, and the I AM. The unrighteous will be cast into the lake of fire.

Both visions were given to give us a clear view of what will happen on judgment day. Believe, friend, and rejoice in the I AM.

First Vision—Daniel 7:1–6, 15–17

In the first year of Belshazzar [Nebuchadnezzar's Grandson] king of Babylon, Daniel had a dream and visions of his head while on his bed. Then he wrote down the dream, telling the main facts.

Daniel spoke, saying, "I saw in my vision by night, and behold, the four winds of heaven were stirring up the Great Sea.

And four great beasts came up from the sea, each different from the other.

The first was like a lion, and had eagle's wings. I watched till its wings were plucked off; and it was lifted up from the earth and made to stand on two feet like a man, and a man's heart was given to it.

"And suddenly another beast, a second [one], like a bear. It was raised up on one side, and had three ribs in its mouth between its teeth. And they said thus to it: 'Arise, devour much flesh!'

"After this I looked, and there was another [one], like a leopard, which had on its back four wings of a bird. The beast also had four heads, and dominion was given to it. . . .

"I, Daniel, was grieved in my spirit within my body, and the visions of my head troubled me.

I came near to one [an angel], of those who stood by and asked him the truth of all this. . . . He told me and made known to me the interpretation of these things:

'Those great beasts, which are four, are four kings which arise out of the earth.

Note: Each beast represents a king who rules over a kingdom. The fourth beast is mentioned below.

Daniel 7:7–8, 21a, 19–20, 23–25, 27–28

[7] "After this I saw in the night visions, and behold, a fourth beast, dreadful and terrible, exceedingly strong. It had huge iron teeth; it was devouring, breaking in pieces, and trampling the residue with its feet. It was different from all the beasts [the three beasts] that were before it, and it had ten horns. [8] I was considering the horns, and there was another horn, a little one, coming up among them . . . [after] three of the first horns were plucked out by the roots. And there, in this horn, were eyes like the eyes of a man, and a mouth speaking pompous words.

44

21a "I was watching; and the same horn was making war against the saints, and prevailing against them.. . .

19 "Then I wished to know the truth about the fourth beast, which was different from all the others, exceedingly dreadful, with its teeth of iron and its nails of bronze, which devoured, broke in pieces, and trampled the residue with its feet; 20 and [I wished to know the truth about] the ten horns that were on its head, and the other horn which came up . . . [after the] three fell . . . that horn which had eyes and a mouth which spoke pompous words, whose appearance was greater than his fellows. . . .

23 "Thus he [the angel] said:

> 'The fourth beast shall be
> A fourth kingdom on earth,
> Which shall be different from all other kingdoms
> [the three that came before it],
> And shall devour the whole earth,
> Trample it and break it in pieces.
> 24 The ten horns are ten kings
> Who shall arise from this kingdom.
>
> And another [the little horn] shall rise after them;
> He shall be different from the first ones [the first
> three horns],
> And shall subdue [the] three kings.
> 25 He shall speak pompous words against the Most
> High [Christ],
> Shall persecute the saints of the Most High,
> And shall intend to change times and law.

Then the saints shall be given into his hand

For a time and times and half a time. . . .

[27] Then the kingdom and dominion,

And the greatness of the kingdoms under the whole heaven,

Shall be given to the people, the saints of the Most High.

His kingdom is an everlasting kingdom,

And all dominions shall serve and obey Him.'

[28] "This is the end of the account. As for me, Daniel, my thoughts greatly troubled me, and my countenance changed; but I kept the matter in my heart."

Allow the Holy Spirit to make what you just read very simple.

Below is an illustration of Daniel 7:

Lion with eagle's wings	First kingdom: **Babylon**
Bear w/three ribs in his teeth	Second kingdom: **Medes-Persians**
Leopard w/ four heads and wings	Third kingdom: **Grecia** (present-day Greece)
Terrible dreadful beast	Fourth kingdom: **Rome**
Ten horns of fourth beast	**Ten kingdoms**

Below are Scriptures that tell the exact name of each kingdom.

Lion w/eagle's wings	**Babylon** (Dan. 2:38)
Bear w/three ribs in his teeth	**Medes-Persians** (Dan. 5:30, 31, 6:8; 8:20)
Leopard w/ four heads and wings	**Grecia** (present-day Greece; Dan. 8:21–22) **Alexander the Great** was the first king of Grecia and is, therefore, the great horn. The four heads of the leopard, the "four stood up," and the areas they ruled are: • **Ptolemy:** Egypt, Palestine, and parts of Syria • **Cassander:** Macedonia w/nominal sovereignty over Greece • **Lysimachus:** Thrace and parts of Asia Minor • **Seleucus:** A large part of the Persian Empire and parts of Asia Minor This era was considered to be a Greco-Macedonian-Asiatic world united by Greek thought and language.
Terrible dreadful beast	**Rome** (Dan. 7:7, 23) Rome was the world power that succeeded Greece and is the world power that operated in the New Testament era.
Ten horns on the fourth beast	**Represent ten kingdoms** (Dan. 7:24) After Alexander's death, Rome was divided into ten separate kingdoms, which were successive Germanic invasions of the Roman Empire: Ostrogoths, Visigoths, Franks, Vandals, Suevi, Alamanni, Anglo-Saxons, Heruli, Lombards, Burgundians

Daniel 7:8, 24:

The "three plucked up" in Daniel 7:8 are the same "subdued three kings" of Daniel 7:24. Daniel 7: 24 informs us that out of the ten kingdoms, three of them were plucked up by a little horn that was different from the original ten. Let us take a closer look at this.

FIRST THREE, NOW ONE

The Heruli, Vandals, and Ostrogoths each were supporters of Arianism. Arianism is a religious doctrine written by Arius stating that Jesus was created by the Father and was not co-eternal with the Father or divine as the Father is. In simple terms, they believed Jesus was only a man and was not God—Jesus was not immortal and lacked divinity, or the nature of God.

Therefore, the overthrow of Rome by the Vandals in 439, the Heruli in 476, and the Ostrogoths in 493 threatened the Roman Church beliefs more than it did the Roman Empire. The Roman Church, as today, functioned as an independent power. The Roman Empire exercised political rule, while the Roman Church exercised ecclesiastical rule. They functioned independently of each other. The invasion and conquest of Rome by the three little horns posed a great threat to the Roman Church by removing their ecclesiastical doctrines and replacing them with Arianism. Both Arianism and Catholicism fought to conquer as much land as possible to gain worldwide power through religious dominance.

In 534, when Belisarius fought against the Ostrogoths, the Ostrogoths, in 538, withdrew from Rome, and it was at that time that the last of the three horns was "plucked up" by the little horn, the

Roman Catholic Church, which is the little horn that rose out of the Roman Empire. Daniel 2:24 states, "Another shall arise" after the ten and "shall subdue the three kings." The Roman Catholic Church rose to power after the former ten kings and did, in fact, subdue the Heruli, Vandals, and Ostrogoths.

HISTORICAL INTERPRETATION OF THE LITTLE HORN

"Out of the ruins of political Rome, arose the great moral Empire in the giant form of the Roman Church."[1]

The Roman Church is the little horn that came up out of the Roman Empire.

"Under the Roman Empire the popes had no temporal powers. But when the Roman Empire had disintegrated and its place had been taken by a number of rude, barbarous kingdoms, the Roman Catholic church not only became independent of the states in religious affairs but dominated secular affairs as well. At times, under such rulers as Charlemagne (768–814), Otto the Great (936–73), and Henry III (1039–56), the civil power controlled the church to some extent; but in general, under the weak political system of feudalism, the well-organized, unified, and centralized church, with the pope at its head, was not only independent in ecclesiastical affairs but also controlled civil affairs."[2]

Do you now see the influence the Catholic Church had in Rome and, as Mr. Eckhardt points out, the pope as the head of this new, unified body called the Catholic Church? This is very important to understand because from the time of Babylon to our present day, the devil was and is using these kingdoms to advance his earthly agenda against God and us. The kingdom the enemy is now using to advance his agenda is the one the papacy heads. The pope is the one who now facilitates Satan's agenda on earth. According to the interpretation of Nebuchadnezzar's dream, Rome became divided. This is understood by the mixing of the iron and clay and means that on one side Rome operates as a government power, while on the other side, it operates as a religious power (Vatican City). Vatican City was birthed out of Rome but is not distinctly separate from it. Since this mixing of the iron and clay is the legs, feet, and toes of the statue, know that we are living in the toenails of this prophecy and must pay close attention to how the devil will work through the papacy. Saints, it's time to spiritually suit up and be filled with the Holy Ghost and enriched with holiness to get ready for what is about to come.

Taking a Closer Look at the "Little Horn"—the Roman Catholic Church

In 533, Emperor Justinian wrote two official letters stating the pope is the "head of all the holy churches" and "head of all the holy priests of God."[3] In addition, he states that the pope is the one who corrects all heretics and exercises political power. This letter gave room and authority to the papacy to gain territorial rule and religious dominance in Europe.

Why is this significant for us? Historical documents also identify the little horn as the pope. Let us read what Daniel 7:8 and 7:11 have to say about the pope. Daniel states, "I considered the horns, and, behold there came up among them another *little horn* . . . and, behold, in this horn were eyes like the *eyes of a man*, and a mouth speaking great things...because of the voice of the great words which the horn spake: I beheld even till *the **beast** was slain*, and . . . given to the burning flame."

Notice three trademarks of the little horn from the above text. First, he is a man ("eyes of a man"); second, he will burn in hell; and third, he is called a "beast." Let us look to Revelation 13:18 for clarity on the first point. "Here is wisdom. Let him that hath understanding count the number of *the **beast**: for it is the number of a **man**; and his number is *Six hundred threescore and six*."

Joe Crews in his book *The Beast, The Dragon and The Woman* interprets Revelation 13:18 by revealing the meaning associated with the Roman numerals written on the pope's miter. Spiritually receive this unveiled wisdom. When the pope is named the "head of all the holy churches . . . and priest of God" the official title given to him is Vicarius Filii Dei. This was inscribed on his miter. Although this title is no longer seen on his miters, these words are a part of every coronation service. When a numerical value is given to each roman numeral, the words add up to 666.

See below:

V — 5	F 0	D — 500
I — 1	I — 1	E — 0
C — 100	L — 50	I 1
A — 0	I — 1	
R — 0	I — 1	
I — 1		
U OR V — 5		
S — 0		
112 +	53 +	501

= 666

Now that we are thoroughly convinced that the little horn is the pope and that the pope is scripturally identified as the beast, let us turn our attention to another verse in Revelation 13. But before we do, I'd like to do a short recap of the material.

Remember, our venture started in Daniel 2 with Nebuchadnezzar's dream of a great statue. Each part of the statue represents a kingdom that would rise to overtake the former kingdom. The statue also represents a succession of kingdoms the devil utilizes to advance his agenda on earth. Here are the kingdoms in order:

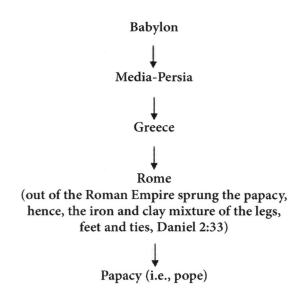

Babylon

↓

Media-Persia

↓

Greece

↓

Rome
(out of the Roman Empire sprung the papacy, hence, the iron and clay mixture of the legs, feet and ties, Daniel 2:33)

↓

Papacy (i.e., pope)

As you can see, we are currently living in the time associated with the feet of Daniel's prophecy—we are living in the tail end of this prophecy, the period that precedes Christ's coming! Hallelujah!!

So that we may become spiritually equipped to stand in the last days, let us look to Revelation 13:1–2 and read what it says about the pope, the beast revealed in Daniel 7.

> And I [John] stood upon the sand of the sea, and saw a beast rise up out of the sea, having seven heads and ten horns, and upon his horns were ten crowns, and upon his head the name of blasphemy. And the beast which I saw was like unto a leopard, and his feet were as the feet of a bear, and his mouth as the mouth of a lion: and the dragon [Satan] gave him his power, and his seat, and great authority.
>
> – Revelation 13:1–2

Wow, this is a lot to digest. First, notice that the beast mentioned here is the same beast mentioned in Daniel 7. The difference is when God gave Daniel the interpretation of Nebuchadnezzar's dream in Daniel 2, He expounded on that prophecy by giving Daniel four other versions of that same dream. The other versions are written in Daniel 7, 8, 10, and 11. The same is true for Revelation 13. God now gives John another version of Nebuchadnezzar's dream that specifically deals with the time period associated with the feet of the statue (Dan. 2:42–43; 8:23). John's vision, unlike Daniel's vision, is revealed to demonstrate how this one beast, the little horn (the papacy), also has the characteristics of the other three beasts. These characteristics confirm how this prophecy is connected to Nebuchadnezzar's dream.

UNDERSTANDING REVELATION 13:1-2

Before we proceed, we must first understand the prophetic vocabulary mentioned in these verses.

1. **Waters/Seas** represent people. Revelation 17:15: "the waters which thou saw . . . are peoples, and multitudes, and nations, and tongues."

2. **Seven heads and ten horns** represent the four beasts in Daniel 7:4-8. The third beast has four heads, making a total of seven heads (four heads plus the remaining three heads equal seven).

3. The **ten horns** represent ten kings: Revelation 17:12. "And the ten horns . . . are ten kings"

4. The words "having seven heads and ten horns" and "was like unto a leopard, and his feet were as the feet of a bear, and his mouth as the mouth of a lion" demonstrate how this beast is a single body with the characteristics of all four beasts mentioned in Daniel 7:4-8.

   - Ten horns and ten crowns = Fourth beast in Daniel 7:7. It had ten horns (Rome/papacy)
   - Like unto a leopard = Third beast in Daniel 7:3, a leopard with four wings and four heads (Greece).
   - Feet of a bear = Second beast in Daniel 7:5. The bear had three ribs and two horns (Media-Persia).
   - Mouth of a lion = First beast in Daniel 7:4. The lion had eagle's wings (Babylon).

SPIRITUAL MEANING OF REVELATION 13:1–2

When John "saw a beast rise up out of the sea, having seven heads," prophetically this means the seven-headed beast came out of a multitude of people—the multitude of people that made up the four kingdoms of Babylon, Media-Persia, Greece, and Rome. Because this single beast is made up of the characteristics of all four beasts, this symbolizes that it is one unit and that all four kingdoms are a single organized system.

Since the last kingdom is Rome, and out of Rome rose the papacy, it is spiritually concluded that the organization that rose out of the fourth beast is the Roman Catholic Church. Therefore, the pope is the beast that rose out of the kingdoms Satan used to set up this church, the Roman Catholic Church. Understand, friend, the Enemy of all creation used Babylon, Media-Persia, Greece, and Rome to give rise to the papacy for the establishment of the Roman Catholic Church.

Hear again the word as it pertains to this beast, the papacy. The Holy Spirit in Revelation 13:2 says, "The dragon gave him [papacy] his power, and his seat, and great authority." With this verse, the Spirit directly connects the papacy to the devil by informing that the devil gives the papacy his position, power, and authority. Wow! Hence, the only reason the devil worked through Babylon, Media-Persia, Greece, and Rome was to give rise to the Catholic Church to give power and authority to the pope.

If you're not yet convinced that the beast is the pope, let's continue with Revelation 13:3:

I saw one of his heads as it were wounded to death; and his deadly wound was healed.

Out of the kingdoms we've studied, from Babylon to Rome, only one horn suffered a blow and was restored back to power. This horn is the papacy. In 1798, the head of the French army, Berthier, entered Rome, took the pope to France as his prisoner and, thus, ended the pope's reign. This was a big blow to the Roman Catholic organization. Territories were lost, and papal power declined. But in 1929, the Lateran Treaty restored temporal power to the pope and rule of Vatican City. Hence, his deadly wound was healed.

Now let us discover two reasons why the Enemy instituted the papacy. The first reason is found in Daniel 7:19–20, 23:

> Then I would know the **truth** of the fourth beast, which was diverse from all others, exceeding dreadful . . . which devoured, break in pieces, and stamped the residue with his feet; And of the ten horns [Ostrogoths and so on] that were in his head,...[one] which came up [little horn/papacy] . . . [when] before . . . three fell [the Heruli, Vandals, and Ostrogoths]; even of that horn [papacy] that had eyes, and a mouth that spake very great things, whose look was more stout than his fellows. . . . The fourth beast shall be the fourth kingdom upon earth, which shall be diverse from all kingdoms [Vatican City is diverse from all other kingdoms], and shall devour the whole earth, and shall tread it down, and break it in pieces.

There is one major point, and it is understood through the phrase "shall devour the whole earth, and shall tread it down, and break it in pieces." It is for that reason the Enemy set up the papacy.

56

But let us compare these words with the words the LORD spoke to Satan in Isaiah 14:17. It reads, "[Satan] made the world as a wilderness, and destroyed the cities."

Can you see how Satan's agenda is being carried out through the papacy? Not convinced? The Greek word for *catholic* is *katholiko*. It means "universal." So, the original meaning of the word *catholic* is "universal," and the Roman Church took on this name centuries ago to demonstrate how it was a religious organization seeking "universal" dominance. The word *Catholic* has no spiritual significance. Rather, it defines the church's agenda for worldwide dominance.

The second reason is found in Revelation 13:3–4. But before we dissect it, please hear what Daniel says in Daniel 7:11: "I beheld then because of the voice of the great words which the horn [papacy] spake: I beheld even till the beast [pope] was slain." Notice that the little horn [pope] is referred to as a beast. This is important to remember as we move forward to Revelation 13:3–4. It reads:

> And all the world wondered after the beast [pope]. And they worshipped the dragon [Satan] which gave power unto the beast [pope]: and they worshipped the beast [pope], saying "Who is like unto the beast [pope]? Who is able to make war with him [the pope]?

Family, the second reason is worship. Satan uses the Catholic Church to turn the world's worship from the Godhead to the papacy to ultimately him. This is sinister. This is blasphemous. This is not only sin but also a spiritual sin. Therefore, whoever gives their allegiance to Satan is committing a spiritual sin.

Spiritual sins are different from carnal sins. This spiritual sin is the highest form of spiritual treason an angel or human can commit against the Godhead. Can you see how spiritually wicked and backward Satan's agenda is? It is maliciously perverse and hideous that he hides behind the establishment of a church, wants to be worshiped, and desires for sinners to commit spiritual treason. He is shrouding his agenda behind a church and used the identity of a church to give rise to worship of himself. This is the most wickedly cunning ploy of the Enemy. Know, therefore, that the establishment of the Catholic Church is a smoke screen—but an intentional, satanic smoke screen. It is a sneaky diversion Satan is using to lure people to worship him to then cause them to commit spiritual treason against God.

Family, we were first created and then redeemed *from sin* to worship the Godhead. We are in no way to give our allegiance to Satan. One profound work of the Holy Spirit is to separate us from Satan and to hand us over to the Father. Since the Holy Spirit is God, know that He, the Holy Spirit, wants us! The Holy Spirit fights for us! He separates us from every work of the enemy to give us freedom to live saved lives. He does not want us to be in league with Satan.

I ask you, therefore, who is this fallen angel that he should boldly work against the Holy Ghost? Who is this fallen angel that he should challenge the Godhead's omnipotence? And who is this fallen angel that thinks that the Godhead will not defend their sovereign headship as God? Satan will burn. He will burn in a vehement flame fueled by their wrath.

Revelation 13:2 says the dragon (Satan) gave the beast (the papacy) his seat, power, and great authority. Now, if the pope receives his power from the devil, what spirit is living in him? And what spirit is working through him? It is surely not the Holy Spirit. It is scripturally concluded that the Catholic Church was formed by Satan and that the pope is filled with an unclean spirit.

One more point the Spirit will mention before He reveals to us how He will solve this spiritually wicked problem. In Bible prophecy, a church is symbolized as a woman. Revelation 12:13 records how Satan "persecuted the woman which bought forth the man child." This means Satan persecuted the first-century church that gave birth to Christ, and he vehemently did so, beginning in the book of Acts (first-century church) continuing through the fourth century (Christian church) and down to our present day (protestant church). Another example is how Christ often referred to backsliding Israel as a harlot (an unclean *woman*).

Now that we know the word *woman* in Bible prophecy means "church," let us turn our attention to Revelation 17:3–6. Hear the Word:

> He [a holy angel] carried me [John] away in the spirit into the wilderness: and I saw a woman [church] sit upon a scarlet coloured beast, full of names of blasphemy, having seven heads and ten horns.
>
> – v. 3

Family, this verse tells us that a church is sitting on a seven-headed beast. This is the same beast of Revelation 13 and the four beasts of Daniel 7:4–7. Since the Roman Catholic Church was birthed out of the fourth beast, this church is the woman sitting on this seven-headed, scarlet-colored beast (Babylon, Media-Persia, Greece, and Rome).

> And the woman was arrayed in purple and scarlet colour, and decked with gold and precious stones and pearls, having a golden cup in her hand full of abominations and filthiness of her fornication.
>
> – v. 4

Here we are told how the Catholic Church's abominations and fornications made her rich and lavish. Thus, the church's outward appearance is a cover-up to disguise how treacherous she really is.

> And upon her forehead was a name written, MYSTERY, BABYLON THE GREAT, THE MOTHER OF HARLOTS [Mother of other false religions] AND ABOMINATIONS OF THE EARTH [God calls the Catholic Church an abomination of the earth because it was established by Satan].
>
> – v. 5

Most importantly, can you see how the Lord has linked this church back to Nebuchadnezzar's dream? He calls the Catholic Church Babylon. Babylon was the first kingdom Satan used to lay the groundwork that ultimately gave rise to it. Not only so, but this verse makes it clear that the church is an abomination. It is rejected by God.

> And I saw the woman drunken with the blood of the saints, and with the blood of the martyrs of Jesus: and when I saw her, I wondered with great admiration.
>
> – v. 6

This verse points out one of her abominations by saying she killed Christians. Remember the crusades and how she persecuted Christians in Europe leading up to the Reformation and later?

Bringing It All Together

> And there appeared another wonder in heaven; and behold a great red dragon [Satan], having seven heads and ten horns, and seven crowns upon his head.
>
> – Revelation 12:3

Let us break this Scripture apart.

"And there appeared another wonder in heaven; and behold a great red dragon,"

The dragon represents Satan.

"having seven heads"

The seven heads are:

- Babylon *(1 head)*
- Media-Persia *(1 head – they ruled jointly)*
- Greece *(4 heads)*
- Rome *(1 head)*

"and ten horns…"

The ten horns are the Ostrogoths and the other nine Germanic invaders.

"and seven crowns upon his head."

The seven crowns belong to:

- Nebuchadnezzar *(1 crown)*
- Cyrus and Darius *(1 crown; Cyrus and Darius jointly ruled Media-Persia),*
- Ptolemy *(1 crown)*
- Cassander *(1 crown)*   Greece was divided into four separate kingdoms
- Seleucus *(1 crown)*
- Lysimachus *(1 crown)*
- The pope *(1 crown)*

Oh, boy!

I ask you to spiritually discern what the Spirit is saying. Here the Spirit openly gives us the connection Satan has with Babylon, Media-Persia, Greece, Rome, and the papacy by revealing that the dragon [Satan] has possession of those kingdoms. He owns them. They belong to him. How do we know? The text says, "A great red dragon *having* seven heads." Notice the word *having*. This word indicates that the devil is in possession of those kingdoms. They are his. They, therefore, are the kingdoms he uses to persuade the whole world to reject God. Therefore, let us discern his work in a more detailed way.

In Revelation 13:1–2, our first image of the beast had seven heads and ten horns. On his horns were ten crowns. The beast was like a leopard, his feet were like a bear, his mouth was like a lion, and the dragon (Satan) gave him (the beast) his power, his seat, and great authority. This means the fourth beast of Daniel 7:7 is connected to the kingdoms that came before it and has the characteristics of those kingdoms. Rome is the first phase of Satan's plan.

The second image of this same beast is of a woman (church) sitting on a scarlet-colored beast with seven heads and ten horns. Here the beast is identified as a church. The Roman Catholic Church is the second phase of Satan's plan.

The third image of the same beast is of a great red dragon (Satan) that has seven heads and ten horns, with seven crowns on his head. Christ is informing us that, from the very start, Satan was in control of the seven heads and ten horns, the four kingdoms represented in Nebuchadnezzar's dream: Babylon, Media-Persia, Greece, and Rome. Thus, the Roman Catholic Church is indisputably Satan's work. The pope, without a doubt, works for him. The third phase of Satan's plan is to use the Catholic Church as an organization to facilitate him being reverenced as a god on earth. Rightly did Christ say Satan "corrupted thy [his] wisdom" (Ezek. 28:17).

Friend of God, can you clearly see the truth about Satan and his work that the Father is unveiling to us? Notice how the seven heads and ten horns are in each phase of Satan's plan to unambiguously show us that they are the same prophecy but just different versions. What more does God have to say?

Since the dragon [Satan] has seven heads and ten horns, the Father is exposing how Satan, from the beginning, planned to use those four kingdoms. This verse tells us that Satan used a succession of kingdoms to advance his hideous agenda on earth. What is the rest of his agenda? It is to make this world desolate and take humanity to hell. Satan wants all life to die because he will die. This is his plan. This is what he has purposed in his heart. This is what he used

Babylon, Media-Persia, Greece, Rome, and Catholicism and the pope for. This is the final phase of his plan.

But will this happen?

Some think Satan's plan is more elaborate than this. I don't believe it is. Yes, every world power is fighting for universal dominance and the oil in the Middle East. But why do you think the Enemy has put an obsession for power and money in the heart of world leaders? It is to blind them to then prompt them to use war—to kill life. The Enemy could care less about our earthly possessions like oil, money, fame, political status, and so on. What are those to him? He is a spiritual creature, a fallen angel. This earth and its traditions and customs were not created for him. Earth was made for humanity, not for fallen angels. He cares nothing about what the earth has to offer. The earth is not as glorious as heaven, where he once lived. Therefore, the riches and power of this world do not entice fallen angels. For this reason, Satan tempts world leaders and us, not to satisfy our greed for money, power, and status but to use those vices to get us to kill life. Satan will use any means necessary to kill life. Again, this earth means nothing to him. His sole plan for humanity is genocide. Hear the Word: "The thief [Satan] comes only to steal [us from Christ] and kill [us] and destroy [the earth]" (John 10:10 ESV).

WILL YOU BELIEVE?

When the devil prompted Eve to sin, what did he say to her? "Ye shall *not* surely *die*" (Gen. 3:4). From the start, Satan intended to kill humanity. He wanted Eve to die. He wanted her to suffer his same consequence. Still not convinced? Then look at the story of Cain and Abel. The Enemy put it in Cain's heart to kill—to kill Abel. Are you persuaded yet? Look at the story of Christ. The devil continuously put murder in man's heart to kill Christ. And why did Christ come? He came to *save us from death.* Thus, the Enemy did not want us to receive a second chance at living. He wanted Christ to die so that humanity would die also.

Therefore, know that there are two ways the Enemy has devised a plan to kill humanity. The first way is to have the world worship the beast. Why? Because God's judgment is against the beast and all who worship the beast. Hear the Word:

> Babylon [the Catholic church] the great is fallen, is fallen, and become the habitation of devils, and the hold of every foul spirit...Come out of her my people, that ye be not partakers of her sins, and that ye receive not of her plagues.
>
> – Revelation 18:2, 4

Family, can you hear God plead with us to live and not die? Can you hear Him plead with us to separate ourselves from Satan's work? Understand that the Godhead is against every satanic work the devil devised through those four kingdoms and is asking for those who have ears to hear and understand this prophecy to come out of Babylon. Come out of the Roman Catholic organization because it is the habitation of devils and every foul spirit.

Family, I sympathize that we see the Catholic organization as a sacred religious body and that the church has presented itself as a righteous institution. But who will you trust? God or the Roman Catholic organization? Will you believe the Lord's report? Will you yield to the understanding of His prophecy? Or will you give way to your own understanding? I only ask that you pray before you answer those questions.

The second way the enemy devised to bring death on humanity is to lead us to sin. The Word says: "The wages of sin is death" (Rom. 6:23). The devil, knowing that God will bring retribution for sin, seeks to entangle each of us in sin, just to have us die an eternal death. This is one reason why confession, forgiveness, and repentance are vital practices of the Christian faith. Firmly recognize that the first way is that the devil will entrap those who follow the pope. The second way is to entrap everyone with sin. Can you agree now how it is Satan's plan to kill us to prevent us from going to glory?

There is much literature written on the Catholic Church and its Babylonian practices. Therefore, if what you have learned so far is not enough to convince you, then I cautiously ask you to research history. But again, I caution you to not get caught up in much learning of the Babylonian rituals present in the Catholic Church, how its doctrines are fused with customs dating back to pagan Rome, and its connection with the Illuminati. Taking on much dark information of this sort can be dangerous to the soul, as it may incite fanaticism. If fanaticism enters the soul, it will shift your attention from Christ and onto the subject you are researching.

I know some people who are fanatics about this subject who don't realize that God's love is not present in their teachings. Nothing should take the place of God's love. They don't realize that they have replaced preaching Christ with preaching the blasphemy of the Catholic Church. Preaching against the Catholic Church will not save souls; only preaching and teaching Christ will. If we are to learn a subject, we are to grasp it in the context of God giving us information to cause us to not be deceived so that we will consciously make the right decision to remain firm in Christ. Alleluia!

Family, my prayer is that you abound in Christ, that you be filled with the Holy Ghost, and that through this in-filling, you will move forward in the Spirit to mature into mighty men, women, and children of holiness, a holiness so humble and brilliant that all who come in contact with you will know you are in perfect relationship with the Father, Son, and Holy Ghost. This is the whole purpose of understanding Nebuchadnezzar's dream. We are to become conscious of every demonic occurrence that seeks to interfere with us becoming one with the Godhead. The Father sent us prophets to inform us of His plans and of the Enemy's plans. Therefore, thanks be to the all-wise God that we are informed Christians.

PART III

THE FATHER AT WORK

Let us take time to behold how mighty and majestic our God is and how He will solve this spiritually wicked problem. Daniel 2:44 will teach us how God was and is currently at work:

> And in the days of these kings [seven heads and ten horns] shall the God of heaven set up a kingdom [Alleluia!], which shall never be destroyed: and the kingdom shall not be left to other people, but it shall break in pieces and consume all these kingdoms [seven heads and ten horns], and it shall stand for ever.

The words "in the days of these kings [the seven heads and ten horns] shall the God of heaven set up a kingdom" allude to how the Father set up His kingdom during the same time Satan worked through Babylon, Media-Persia, Greece, and Rome. The phrase "which shall never be destroyed" signifies how the Father's kingdom will not be overthrown by Satan's kingdom, and "it shall stand forever" denotes how the Father's kingdom is eternal. The words "shall break in pieces and consume all these kingdoms" inform us how God's kingdom will destroy Satan's work as orchestrated through Babylon, Media-Persia, Greece, Rome, and the Catholic organization and the pope. And the words "the kingdom shall not be left to other men" is pregnant with meaning. We will flesh that part out later in the reading.

Alleluia. Let's begin!

In Daniel 8, we read about a ram with two horns and a male goat with a single horn that broke off and was replaced by four other horns then replaced again with a little horn. For the interpretation of the ram and the goat, we need to turn our attention to Daniel 8:20–21:

> [20] The ram which thou saw having two horns are the kings of Media [Darius] and Persia [Cyrus].
>
> [21] And the rough goat is the king of Grecia [Greece]: and the great horn that is between his eyes is the first king [Alexander the Great].

Now let us look closely at the horn [king, Alexander the Great] associated with the goat. Hear Daniel 8:7–9:

> And I saw him [Alexander the Great] come close unto the ram [Media-Persia], and he was moved with choler [anger] against him, and smote the ram [Media-Persia], and brake his two horns [king Darius and king Cyrus]: and there was no power in the ram [Media-Persia] to stand before him [Alexander the Great], but he cast him down to the ground, and stamped upon him: and there was none that could deliver the ram [Media-Persia] out of his [Alexander the Great] hand.

Therefore the he goat [Greece] waxed very great: and when he was strong, the great horn [Alexander the Great] was broken; and for it [and in place of it] came up four [Ptolemy, Cassander, Lysimachus, and Seleucus] notable ones.

And out of one of them [Cassander] came forth a little horn [papacy], which waxed exceeding great, toward the south [Egypt], and toward the east [Seleucid Empire], and toward the pleasant land [Jerusalem].

As we move forward, remember there is a spiritual element to this prophecy. In Daniel 10:12–13, we learned that a holy angel was confronted by a fallen angel Satan appointed to rule over Persia. That fallen angel is called a territorial spirit. We also learned how the holy angel received help from Michael, a chief prince over God's holy angels. This means a spiritual battle was in process and continued until Greece succeeded Media-Persia. How do we know? Daniel 10:20 informs how this same holy angel told Daniel that he had to "return to fight with the prince of Persia [the territorial spirit]" and afterward, "the prince of Grecia"—another fallen angel assigned over that territory—"would come."

Do you now believe Satan has assigned ranking fallen angels to govern his kingdoms and that God is currently engaged in spiritual battles because of this? Therefore, let us get another glimpse of this same spiritual battle as it relates to what will happen after Rome succeeds Greece.

Hear Daniel 8:10–12:

> And it [the pope] waxed great, even to the host of heaven;
> and it [the pope] cast down some of the host and of the
> stars to the ground and stamped upon them.

> Yea, he magnified himself even to the prince of the host,
> and by him the daily sacrifice was taken away, and the place
> of the sanctuary was cast down.

> And an host was given him against the daily sacrifice by
> reason of transgression, and it cast down the truth to the
> ground.

The words "he magnified himself even to the prince of the host"
are best understood when read with Daniel 8:23–25. Hear the text:

> And in the latter time of their kingdom [Rome], when the
> transgressors are come to the full, a king [pope] of fierce
> countenance, and understanding dark sentences [he
> communicates with Satan], shall stand up.

> And his power shall be mighty, but not by his own power
> [Rev. 13:4 states that Satan gives the pope his power]: and
> he shall destroy wonderfully, and shall prosper, and
> practice, and shall destroy the mighty and the holy people.

> And through his policy also he shall cause craft [witchcraft]
> to prosper in his hand; and he shall magnify himself in his
> heart, and by peace shall destroy many: he shall also stand
> up against the Prince of princes [Christ]; but he shall be
> broken without hand.

Alleluia!

These texts teach how the pope is in league with the Adversary to have a continual supply of satanic power and that he exalts himself up against the holy angels and against the Prince of princes—Christ. The passage also enlightens us as to how the pope will use peace to destroy—kill life. But amid this prophetic revelation, Daniel 8:13–14 says:

> Then I heard one saint speaking, and another saint said unto that certain saint which spake, How long shall be the vision concerning the daily sacrifice, and the transgression of desolation, to give both the sanctuary and the host to be trodden under foot? And he said unto me, Unto two thousand and three hundred days [2,300 days]; then shall the sanctuary be cleansed.

Alas! We are now about to see our God work marvelously! The words "daily sacrifice, and the transgression of desolation" point to the same event. The above saints understood that this chaos will near its end sometime after the 2,300 days. Christ gives clarity to this in Matthew 24:15 when He told the people what will happen in the last days. He cautioned them by saying, "When ye therefore shall see the abomination of desolation, spoken of by Daniel the prophet, stand in the holy place." Wow! The words "Daniel the prophet," "abomination of desolation," and "transgression of desolation" inform that we are studying the right prophecy in preparation for last-day events.

After the vision of Daniel 8, Daniel prays. Chapter 9 is the prayer he spoke in response to what God revealed to him. Daniel 9:21–22 says:

> While I was speaking in prayer, even the man Gabriel, whom I had seen in the vision at the beginning, being caused to fly swiftly, touched me. . . . And he informed me, and talked with me, and said, O Daniel, I am now come forth to give thee skill and understanding.

Glory! Family, do you know what this means? The verses that follow will tell us exactly what the Father is doing. Glory, Alleluia!! Hear the angel Gabriel speak in Daniel 9:23–25:

> At the beginning of thy supplications the commandment came forth, and I [Gabriel] am come to show thee; for thou art greatly beloved: therefore understand the matter, and consider the vision.

> Seventy weeks are determined upon thy people [the Jews] and upon thy holy city [Jerusalem], to finish the transgression, and to make an end of sins, and to make reconciliation for iniquity, and to bring in everlasting righteousness, and to seal up the vision and prophecy, and to anoint the most Holy.

> Know therefore and understand, that from the going forth of the commandment to restore and to build Jerusalem unto the Messiah the Prince shall be seven weeks, and threescore and two weeks [7 weeks + 62 weeks = 69 weeks]: the street shall be built again, and the wall, even in troublous times.

Before we dive into this, remember the children of Israel are in Babylonian captivity. According to Jeremiah 29:10, they were in captivity for 70 years, while Jerusalem laid waste. But Gabriel is now telling Daniel two things. One, seventy weeks are determined on the Jews, and two, 69 weeks will lapse between the time Jerusalem is rebuilt until the Messiah. Therefore, the date given to rebuild Jerusalem is the starting date for the 70 weeks and for the 69 weeks.

Though there were many decrees given in the book of Ezra to rebuild Jerusalem, it was the decree of King Artaxerxes I, in the fall of 457 BC, that gave complete restoration to Jerusalem. Therefore, the fall of 457 BC is the starting date of the 70 weeks and of the 69 weeks. In Bible prophecy, Numbers 14:34 states one day equals one year. This means 70 weeks x 7 = 490 days, which in turn, are 490 years. And 69 weeks x 7 = 483 days, which in turn, are 483 years. Therefore, 490 years – 457 years = AD 34 (the fall of AD 34). This means AD 34 is the end date for the 70 weeks. And 483 years – 457 years = AD 27 [the fall of AD 27]. This means AD 27 is the end date for the 69 weeks.

What's the significance? Gabriel alluded to how 483 years after Jerusalem is rebuilt the children of Israel should expect to see something in AD 27 that points to the Messiah. Sure enough, in the fall of AD 27 Christ was baptized. His baptism marks the fulfilment of the 69-week prophecy. Therefore, when John the Baptist saw Jesus coming to be baptized and said, "Behold the Lamb of God which taketh away the sins of the world," he, through those words, confirmed the accuracy of Daniel's prophecy.

Prophetic Timeline Illustration:

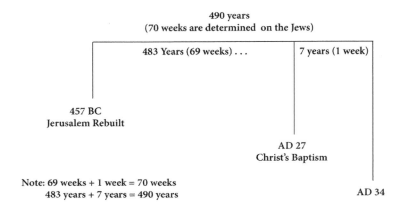

490 years
(70 weeks are determined on the Jews)

483 Years (69 weeks) . . .   7 years (1 week)

457 BC
Jerusalem Rebuilt

AD 27
Christ's Baptism

Note: 69 weeks + 1 week = 70 weeks
483 years + 7 years = 490 years

AD 34

Daniel, in 9:27, expressed something very important and most vital to our salvation that hinges on Christ's baptism. Hear the verse:

And he [Christ] shall confirm the covenant with many for one week [7 years]: and in the *midst of the week* he [Christ] shall cause the sacrifice and the oblation to cease for the overspreading of the abomination he [Christ] shall make it desolate, even until the consummation, and that determined shall be poured out upon the desolate.

The date that starts the "one week [seven years]," is AD 27. The text says that in the midst of that week [the seven years] Christ will cause the sacrifices and oblations to cease. Now if AD 27 starts the one-week, then seven years later is the end date, correct? 27 + 7 = 34, or AD 34. This is no coincidence. Gabriel is saying the mid-point year between AD 27 and AD 34 is the year to expect the sacrifices to cease. Sure enough, in AD 31 Christ was crucified, which is the mid-point year between AD 27 and AD 34. His death is what caused the sacrificial system to cease. The veil in the temple was ripped to symbolize an end to that sacrificial system and the fulfillment of the old covenant, Ten Commandment law. From this, we can determine that the date of Christ's death confirms the dating accuracy of the entire prophecy.

Prophetic Timeline Illustration:

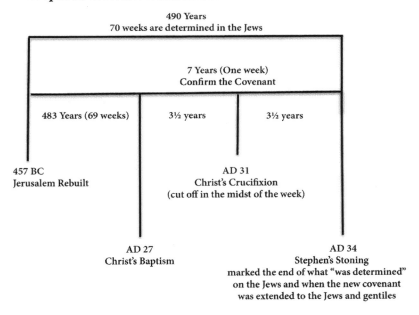

490 Years
70 weeks are determined in the Jews

7 Years (One week)
Confirm the Covenant

483 Years (69 weeks)   3½ years   3½ years

457 BC
Jerusalem Rebuilt

AD 31
Christ's Crucifixion
(cut off in the midst of the week)

AD 27
Christ's Baptism

AD 34
Stephen's Stoning
marked the end of what "was determined"
on the Jews and when the new covenant
was extended to the Jews and gentiles

The Holy Spirit at Work

The one-week portion of the prophecy has strong implications for believers. Gabriel says, Christ will "confirm the covenant with many for one week [for seven years]." In AD 27, Christ began His public ministry after being baptized by John the Baptist. The Scriptures record that the Holy Spirit descended on Him to point to the Holy Spirit as a pivotal functioning presence in Christ's life.

But for what ultimate purpose did the Holy Spirit descend on Christ? Romans 8:2, through the words "the law of the Spirit of life in Christ Jesus," teaches (1) that the Holy Spirit has a law; (2) the Spirit's law produces life; and (3) His law lives in Christ. This means the Holy Spirit descended on Christ to give Christ His law. So that there will be no misunderstanding, let us examine Romans 8:2 in its entirety:

> The law of the Spirit of life in Christ Jesus hath made me free from the law of sin and death.

In this text we see two laws.

1. The law of the Spirit
2. The law of sin

There are two ways we can discern that this text is speaking about two different laws. One way is through the words, "hath made me free." These words indicate that the Holy Spirit's law is different from the law of sin, by way of its power to **set us free** from the law of sin.

The second way is

1. The Holy Spirit's law gives **life**

    but

2. The law of sin gives **death**

I can hear you ask, "What is the law of sin then?" For this answer, we must turn our attention to Romans 7:7:

It reads, "I had not known sin but by the law: for I had not known lust, except the law had said, Thou shalt not covet." The words "Thou shalt not covet" teach us that Paul is talking about the Ten Commandment law. The Ten Commandment law is a list of sins that Paul, in Romans 7:25, refers to as "the law of sin." Not only so, but since the law of sin gives death, understand this to mean that the Ten Commandment law requires us to die—to die daily to sin.

This law will never give us life. It was instituted to kill sin. Therefore, if we are to have life after we have crucified our flesh, the only way to obtain this is through the Holy Spirit's law. It is His law that gives life to us. The most important takeaway from Romans 8:2 is to know that since the Holy Spirit's law lives in Christ, only those who are in Christ are privy to receiving and walking in the Spirit's law. This law is of such great importance to the Godhead that they entrusted it to Christ and not to other men, as the Ten Commandment law was entrusted to Moses. This difference helps to understand how Christ is the testator of a *new* covenant—the Holy Spirit's law—to cause all believers to enter into a *new spiritual covenant* with the Godhead.

Not convinced? Hear Hebrews 8:13, 7, 6, in this order:

> [13] In that he saith, A new covenant, he hath made the first old. Now that which decayeth and waxeth old is ready to vanish away.

> [7] For if that first covenant [Ten Commandment Law] had been faultless, then should no place have been sought for the second [covenant—Holy Spirit's law].

> [6] But now hath he [Christ] obtained a more excellent ministry, by how much also he is the mediator of a better covenant [the Holy Spirit's law], which was established upon better promises.

Alleluia!!

Family, can you hear the Holy Spirit say that Christ is now the Mediator of a new covenant? Can you see how the Holy Spirit is making a distinction between the Ten Commandment law and this new covenant we have come to know as the Holy Spirit's law? The promises attached to the Ten Commandment law are that our sins will be forgiven and that we will not experience the Father's wrath, whereas, the "better promises" attached to the Holy Spirit's law are that we will be born again, we will abound in holiness, we will be restored back to our communion with the Father, Son, and Holy Ghost, and we will live forever. Is this not the Holy Spirit's work toward us? Are not these promises greater than the promises attached to the Ten Commandment law? Therefore, will you willingly believe that Christ's baptism by the Spirit offers us the opportunity to receive the Holy Spirit's law?

DISCERNING THE HOLY SPIRIT'S LAW

Let us center our attention on Matthew 22:34–40 for understanding:

> But when the Pharisees had heard that [Jesus] had put the
> Sadducees to silence, they were gathered together. Then
> one of them, which was a lawyer, asked him a question,
> tempting him, and saying, Master, which is the great
> commandment in the law? Jesus said unto him, Thou shalt
> love the Lord thy God with all thy heart, and with all thy
> soul, and with all thy mind. This is the first and great
> commandment. And the second is like unto it, Thou shalt
> love thy neighbor as thyself. On these two commandments
> hang all the law and the prophets.

Notice how the lawyer expected Christ to mention one of the
laws listed in the Ten Commandments. Instead, Christ answered the
lawyer's question by pointing his attention to the two Great
Commandments. This is significant. Christ wanted the lawyer to
grasp what the greatest commandment is. And though the lawyer
thought that the greatest commandment would be one of the Ten
Commandments, it was not. Instead, it was a different law altogether.

Christ further states that on those "two commandments hang all
the law and the prophets." Wow. Before we move forward to
understand what that means, we must spiritually discern that the two
Great Commandments, since they are centered on love, are what
make up a law called the Law of Love. This Law of Love is the
GREATest commandment.

Secondly, to fully understand what Christ means when He says,
"upon these two [Law of Love] hang all the law and the prophets," we

should understand that the words "all the law" are speaking about the Ten Commandment law and the words "the prophets" are speaking about the Bible (since every book in the Bible is written by a prophet). Therefore, the meaning of Matthew 22:36–40 is this: The Bible and the Ten Commandment law hang on the Law of Love. This means that the Law of Love existed before the Ten Commandment law and the Bible. It also means that the Ten Commandment law and the Bible were both birthed out of the Law of Love. The Law of Love gives strength to the Ten Commandment law and the Bible and is what bears them up. Understand, friend, the Ten Commandment law and the Bible were created and composed out of the Law of Love, and they are completely dependent on the Law of Love for power. Therefore, without the pre-existence of the Law of Love, the Ten Commandment law and the Bible would be powerless to convict and condemn sin.

To better support how the two great commandments are the Holy Spirit's law, let's turn our attention to Galatians 5:22. The first seven words, "The fruit of the Spirit is love" mean only the Holy Spirit can impart love in us. Not only so, but because the Holy Spirit is God and 1 John 4:8 says, "God is love," know that the Holy Spirit as God is love. And since He is love, the Father is love. And because Jesus came in the Father's image as love, know that they as one LORD are love. Therefore, love is the law of their kingdom because it is who they are. The Law of Love, not the Ten Commandment law, is the exact image of their character. It is the image we are born again to resemble. We are not born again to resemble the Ten Commandment law. Rather, we are born again to look exactly like the Law of Love—the Godhead's image. It is profoundly spiritually concluded that the Law of Love is the Holy Spirit's law. It is the law the Holy Spirit gave Christ at His baptism.

This is important to know for two reasons. One, Daniel 9:27 states, "[Christ] shall confirm the covenant with many for one week [seven years]." If the "one week" starts at Christ's baptism and involves Christ's crucifixion and resurrection and ends at Stephen's death, then **what** Christ will confirm has to do with the Holy Spirit's law. The Holy Spirit, therefore, gave Christ His law, not the Ten Commandment law, to confirm that law with us. The Ten Commandment law is a list of sins God wrote to tell us what Christ died for and what He forgives us for. The Ten Commandment law is a law of reconciliation and a law of atonement. But the Holy Spirit's law is a law of confirmation, the law He gives to confirm the Spirit has imparted their love in us and to confirm His love toward us and our love toward them. Because of this, it is decided that the Holy Spirit's law is the new covenant law we are to receive to display that we are changing into their image and abiding in their image—love.

Prophetic Timeline Illustration:

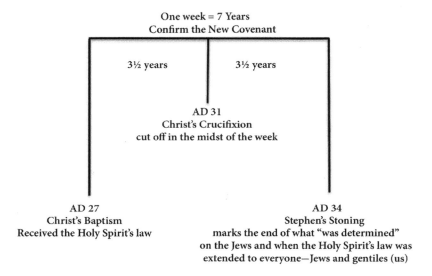

One week = 7 Years
Confirm the New Covenant

3½ years   3½ years

AD 31
Christ's Crucifixion
cut off in the midst of the week

AD 27
Christ's Baptism
Received the Holy Spirit's law

AD 34
Stephen's Stoning
marks the end of what "was determined"
on the Jews and when the Holy Spirit's law was
extended to everyone—Jews and gentiles (us)

It is spiritually safe to say the Holy Spirit's law is the new covenant Christ established during that "one week" to confirm with many. The "many" are not only those living at that time but include believers in our present day and in generations after us up until Christ comes. What does the word say? "Repent . . . and ye shall receive the gift of the Holy Ghost. For the promise is unto you and to your children and all that are afar off, even as many as the LORD our God shall call" (Acts 2:38–39).

Friend of God, the Father and Christ's promise to give us the Holy Spirit is not specifically to have us work signs and wonders. More importantly, they promised us the Holy Spirit to cause us to be born again into their image. This is the highest work of the Holy Spirit extended to humanity. So when you pray to receive the Holy Ghost, would you rather desire that the Holy Ghost cause you to be born again by imparting His law in you? Or would you rather receive a spiritual gift instead? Which is greater? You choose.

I would like to further press the point of Christ receiving the Holy Spirit's law by saying, since He received the Spirit's law at His baptism and at His crucifixion, He atoned for and abolished the Ten Commandment law. This automatically means that on His resurrection He became the mediator of a new covenant—the Holy Spirit's law (see Heb. 8:7–8, 13). This is also the fulfilment of the new covenant that the Holy Spirit declared Christ would make with the "house of Israel and Judah" (Heb. 8:8). Not only so, but Stephen's death marked the moment when this new covenant—the Holy Spirit's law—was extended to us (see Acts 22:21).

My friend, I ask you, when Paul was sent to the gentiles, how was he sent? And what was he sent with? Matthew 3:11 says, "I [John the Baptist] indeed baptize you with water unto repentance: but he [Christ] who comes after me . . . shall baptize you with the Holy Ghost..." This is an important spiritual passage to understand. Since it is Christ who baptizes us with the Holy Spirit, and the Holy Spirit baptized Christ by imparting His law in Him, then it is only right to conclude that when Christ baptizes us with the Holy Ghost, He does so to fill us with the Holy Spirit's law—love.

But before I move forward, family, you must understand that the old covenant was with the house of Israel only and not with the rest of the world. This does not mean that the rest of the world had a license to sin. It only means that the Godhead made a covenant with Israel and worked through them to save the whole world. But now that Christ has fulfilled His covenant with Israel to die for every man's sins, He now can make a new covenant with the whole world without our sins getting in the way. Therefore, when Christ baptized Paul with the Holy Spirit, He did so to impart the Spirit's law in him to cause Paul to abide in the new covenant. And when Paul was sent to the gentiles, he was sent under the new covenant to confirm the Law of Love "with many" through the preaching of the gospel under that law. Friend, understand, the gospel is now preached under the new covenant—the Holy Spirit's law—and not under the old covenant— the Ten Commandment law. Glory to His great name!

If you want to know what the Father is doing *now*, if you want to know how He is building His kingdom *now*, know that He has sent the Holy Spirit to impart His law in us to legitimize us as citizens of His kingdom. When we get to glory's gate, if the Father does not see His love, the Holy Spirit's law, living in us, He will say to us, "I never knew you: depart from me, ye that work iniquity" (Matt. 7:23). Why? Because love is His living proof that we belong to Him. Since it is the Holy Spirit who works love in us, He, the Son, and the Father know what their love looks like and will not be fooled. The Holy Spirit seals us with His Law of Love as living proof that He worked His law in us. Hear Ephesians 1:13: "…After that ye believed, ye were sealed with that holy Spirit of promise." Know again, saints, the work Christ is now confirming with many is to fill and seal us with the Holy Spirit's law—love. This is the LORD's work, and it is marvelous in our sight.

Prophetic Timeline Illustration:

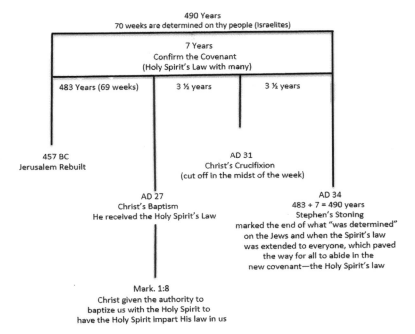

JESUS AT WORK

The second point is to understand what "he [Christ] shall make...desolate, even until the consummation, and that determined shall be poured out upon the desolate" means (Dan. 9:27). The "consummation" occasion and the "poured out upon the desolate" occasion happens to two different groups of people. The latter group are those who will receive God's judgment, "that determined shall be poured out [on them]." The former group is the redeemed. The word *consummation* carries a matrimonial meaning to imply that the sealed people are ready for their marriage to Christ. Let us first

87

discover the scriptural meaning behind "that determined shall be poured out."

That Determined Shall Be Poured Out:

> [8] And there followed another angel, saying, Babylon [Catholic organization/Vatican City] is fallen, is fallen, that great city, because she made all nations drink of the wine of the wrath of her fornication.

> [9] And the third angel followed them, saying with a loud voice, If any man worship the beast and his image, and receive his mark in his forehead, or in his hand,

> [10] The same shall drink of the wine of the wrath of God, which is poured out without mixture into the cup of his indignation; and he shall be tormented with fire and brimstone in the presence of the holy angels, and in the presence of the Lamb:

> [11] And the smoke of their torment ascended up for ever and ever: and they have no rest day nor night, who worship the beast and his image, and whosoever receiveth the mark of his name.

> – Revelation 14:8–11

I beheld till the thrones were cast down, and the Ancient of days did sit, whose garment was white as snow, and the hair of his head like the pure wool: his throne was like the fiery flame, and his wheels as burning fire.

A fiery stream issued and came forth from before him: thousand thousands ministered unto him, and ten thousand times ten thousand stood before him: the judgment was set, **and the books were opened.**

I beheld...because of the voice of the great words which the horn spake [pope]: I beheld even till the beast [pope] was slain, and his body destroyed, and given to the burning flame.

– Daniel 7:9–11

And the beast [pope] was taken, and with him the false prophet that wrought miracles before him, with which he deceived them that had received the mark of the beast, and them that worshipped his image. These both were cast alive into a lake of fire burning with brimstone.

– Revelation 19:20

And the devil that deceived them was cast into the lake of fire and brimstone, where the beast [pope] and the false prophet are, and shall be tormented day and night for ever and ever.

– Revelation 20:10

And I saw the dead, small and great, stand before God; **and the books were opened**: and another book was opened, which is the book of life:

And whosoever was not found written in the book of life was cast into the lake of fire.

– Revelation 20:12, 15

Family, there is one way only that the Father has devised to end the wickedness propagated by Satan, and His way is to burn them up. Satan, the pope, unrighteous people, this earth, the sky, and the atmospheres above it will all burn to give way to the creation of a new heaven and a new earth (see 2 Peter 3:10; Rev. 21:1). Therefore, "he [Christ] shall make...desolate" and "that determined shall be poured out" mean Christ will destroy Satan's works and will kill the fallen angels and all those who follow Satan (1 John 3:8; Heb. 2:14).

TAKING A CLOSER LOOK AT REVELATION 13:11

Then I saw another beast coming up out of the earth, and he had two horns like a lamb and spoke like a dragon [Satan].

And he exercises all the authority of the first beast [the pope] in his presence, and causes the earth and those who dwell in it to worship the first beast [pope], whose deadly wound was healed. . . .

He was granted *power* to give breath to the image of the beast [the pope], that the image of the beast [pope] should both speak and cause as many as would not worship the image of the beast to be killed.

– Revelation 13:11–12, 15 (NKJV)

These texts are rich with information, but we will focus on one point: the beast that rose out of the earth. Notice how the beasts before this one— Babylon, Media-Persia, Greece, and Rome—rose out of the sea. And this beast rises out of the earth. The word "another" is intended to point our attention to a nation that came to power after Rome and not before Rome. Hold on to your seat, family. The world power that rose after Rome is America. What is horrifying is America was first established for religious liberty, a separation of Christianity from Catholicism. The migrants that came here were people who fled persecution from the Roman Catholic Church and understood that the tenets of that organization were not scriptural. The Protestants who fled wanted to worship the living God without retribution from the Catholic Church. But from the fourteenth century till now, an adulterated spiritual shift has taken place in America from Protestant Christian freedom to freedom of other religious practices that include atheism, Satanism, Hinduism, Islam, Taoism, Buddhism, and Confucianism, to name a few. The practice of these religions in America defiles its soil. But the most hideous religion rising is the intermingling of secularism with religion. Some examples are New Age, the Hip Hop Bible, Todd Bentley, the church that held a Beyoncé worship service, and Kanye West Sunday worship services.

Let's stop right here, just for a moment, to reason this through. From the time of the Old Testament till now, has the Holy Spirit ever moved in the ways practiced in the above religions? Has the Holy Spirit ever needed a secular beat or people to roll uncontrollably on the ground to demonstrate worship? Has the Holy Spirit ever needed New Age meditation to reveal Christ to His people? When it comes to the Holy Spirit, there is a distinct difference between the godly and the profane! The rise of these new religious practices are perverse and profane in God's sight!

Hear the Spirit of the living God. This new fusion of masking secularism with supposed religious practices is the image of the beast that America has given birth to. America should have stood her spiritual ground and not allowed her soil to be polluted by false religions like Babylon was. False religions opened the door for Satan to form an image to the pope. Satan is intermingling the secular with religion, just like he did in the fourth century when he merged paganism with Christianity to ultimately give birth to the Catholic Church. As long as paganism and Christianity were separate, it was easy to see the difference between the two. But when Satan merged them by forming Catholicism, it became difficult to discern the pagan rituals cloaked in the church's religious practices.

What Satan is doing now is the same thing he accomplished then. The difference is that the religion he is giving birth to is the rise and acceptance of a foul, unclean spirit, a spirit so foul that it will produce blasphemous worship. The earth will reek of sin. The stench of this worship is proof that it comes from Satan and not God. And because it comes cloaked as a religious organization, it will be accepted as Christian and not as a demonic imitation.

Burn them up, Jesus. Burn them up!

Even Until the Consummation

Ephesians 1:13 states, "After that ye heard . . . the gospel of your salvation . . . ye were sealed with that Holy Spirit of promise"; and Ephesians 4:30 states, "Grieve not the Holy Spirit . . . whereby ye are sealed unto the day of redemption." Both texts express how the final work of the Godhead is the Holy Spirit's work to seal us. Since the Word says, "Unto the [final] day of redemption," this teaches that only those who are sealed with the Holy Ghost are redeemed from the earth to go to glory. The significance behind this is to believe the Holy

Spirit's law is His seal He imparts in us to ready us for our transport to glory. And since His law is love, and He, the Father, and the Son are love, they as love abide in us through the Spirit's law to signify that we belong to them and they to us. Not only so, but since they are love and they are their seal living in us, our sealing cannot be counterfeited. For it is their life living in us to authenticate we are sealed.

To take this a step further, when Paul said, "The Holy Spirit of promise," he meant that the Holy Spirit is the promise the Father gave us. Family, this is good news in that though we received the Ten Commandment law, it was not the promise God spoke to Abraham that we would receive. Glory to Your name, Jesus! The Ten Commandment law paved the way for the Holy Spirit's law to show forth how we would abide in the Father's promise for the Spirit to work in us a holy love to love them with all our heart, mind, soul, and strength and to love our neighbors with their love (see Gal. 3:14). All things are made perfect and one through their love alone—the Spirit's law. This is glorious. This is marvelous. This is the Godhead working their best in us.

Christ says, "Behold, I make all things new" (Rev. 21: 5), to point out how it is through His death and resurrection that all things become new to become governed under the Holy Spirit's law. This is the new thing Isaiah prophesied in 43:19 that Christ would do. Most importantly and more wonderful is that the Holy Spirit's law is the only law of God's kingdom, the sovereign supreme rule of their kingdom. Glory to your name, Holy One.

To have the assurance that we are going to a kingdom governed by love is to know and believe that all things—whatsoever they are—will live, move, and have their being through love, the eternal law of God. Finally, the Holy Spirit, through the impartation of His law, has readied the redeemed for our marriage to Christ. We will turn our attention to Revelation 19:6–9 and 21:1–6 to behold what this consummation ceremony will look like.

> And I heard as it were the voice of a great multitude [you and me—we're there!], and as the voice of many waters [people, nations, and tongues], and as the voice of mighty thunderings, saying, Alleluia: for the Lord God omnipotent reigneth.
>
> Let us be glad and rejoice, and give honour to him: for the marriage of the Lamb [Jesus] is come, and his wife [those who are sealed with the Holy Spirit's law] hath made herself ready.
>
> And to her was granted that she should be arrayed in fine linen, clean and white: for the fine linen [Law of Love] is the righteousness of the saints.
>
> And he saith unto me, Write, Blessed are they which are called unto the marriage supper of the Lamb. And he saith unto me, These are the true sayings of God.
>
> – Revelation 19:6–9
>
> And I saw a new heaven and a new earth: for the first heaven and the first earth were passed away . . .

And I John saw the holy city, new Jerusalem, coming down from God out of heaven, prepared as a bride adorned for her husband.

And I heard a great voice out of heaven saying, Behold, the tabernacle of God is with men, and he will dwell with them, and they shall be his people, and God himself shall be with them, and be their God.

And God shall wipe away all tears from their eyes; and there shall be no more death, neither sorrow, nor crying, neither shall there be any more pain: for the former things are passed away.

And he that sat upon the throne said, Behold, I make all things new. And he said unto me, Write: for these words are true and faithful.

And he said unto me, It is done. I am Alpha and Omega, the beginning and the end. I will give unto him that is athirst of the fountain of the water of life freely.

– Revelation 21:1–6

Family, can you plainly see how the whole purpose of Christ's death is to remove sin out of the way? This gives us the opportunity to receive the Holy Spirit's law, which will prepare us for our union with the Godhead through our marriage to Christ. Just think, family, this is the most glorious gift the Father desires to give us by faith. All we must do is live by faith, confess our sins, and we will receive forgiveness and the Holy Spirit's law and go to glory. Alleluia! All this is granted to us through faith. Faith in the Father, faith in the Son, and faith in the Holy Ghost. We need no money to get to heaven. All we need is faith.

SUMMING IT ALL UP

Let us rejoice in knowing the Father gave Nebuchadnezzar a dream about four kingdoms that foretold how Satan would use these kingdoms to kill life, establish the Catholic Church, give birth to a new religion, and ultimately build an army that would oppose God on the final day of earth's history (Rev. 20:8–9). At this same time, the Father gave His prophets Daniel and John the interpretation of this dream to expose the enemy's plan and to demonstrate how He knows all things and is in control of everything that will happen. For this reason, God gave this prophecy to cause us to take courage in Him and to trust that all is well in His kingdom as we continue to rely on His wisdom and strength to get us to glory.

The most vital component of how the Father will deal with Satan and build His kingdom came in the form of Jesus Christ. Christ's death fulfilled the old covenant law and ushered us into a new covenant with the Almighty, a covenant that was founded on "better promises" to re-create us and fill us with the Holy Spirit's law to then ready us for transport to glory. On the flip side, Christ's death sealed the fate of the fallen angels and those who follow Satan—to have their lives eternally end by fire.

Glory to your name, Jesus. Sin will not rise up a second time!

Lastly, when the Father, in Daniel 2:44, said He will "set up a kingdom, which shall never be destroyed: and the kingdom shall not be left to other people," He hinted to Christ's coronation ceremony.

KEPT BY THE WORD

This is the time when Christ will be acknowledged as the sole heir and King of the redeemed. The redeemed are a kingdom of people who will not be governed by other men like Israel was governed by Saul, David, and so on. Instead, Christ will be coronated as the King of the redeemed, and at this ceremony, Christ will receive His new name. Hear Revelation 3:12 when Christ says, "He [the redeemed] that overcometh. . . I will write upon him my new name."

Family, hold on to your seat; this is pregnant with so much meaning. But, in short, everything under heaven right now is governed under the name *Jesus*. It is through that name that sin is forgiven, demons are cast out, the sick are healed, prophecies are given, and we are sealed with the Holy Ghost. But when sin is eradicated and this earth is burned up, Christ then will receive a new name that the new heaven and the new earth will be governed under. This new name will carry more weight and glory than the name *Jesus*. Alleluia!

Therefore, when Christ is coronated and transitions from being the Son of Man to be the I AM, His new name will evoke a higher level of praise and worship, which all the redeemed, holy angels, and other worlds will experience **together** for the first time. Hear again the Word. At His coronation, all creation for the first time will erupt with one accord to glorify Him, exalt Him, and magnify the wonders of who He is as the splendid brilliance of being God. This very thought makes me want to shout! Come on, let's shout together!

PART IV

ONLY THE FALLEN ANGELS, NOT US

The Holy Spirit will unveil to us three revelations that relate specifically to fallen angels.

FIRST REVELATION—JOHN 8:44

The first revelation is from John 8:44, which reads, "The devil . . . abode not in the truth, because there is no truth in him."

To spiritually discern the significance of this text, we must take time to know who the Holy Spirit is in connection with the fallen angels. Because God is Spirit and angels are spiritual creatures, when Christ calls the fallen angels unclean *spirits*, He again is making a distinction between the nature of their *spirit* in contrast to the nature of God as Spirit. The nature of God as Spirit is holy. Hence, the use of the word *Holy* preceding the word *Spirit*. This arrangement as well as the word *unclean* before the word *angels* clearly reveals that fallen angels do not have a holy spiritual nature.

Holy angels, on the other hand, *do* have a holy spiritual nature. But what makes the spiritual nature of fallen angels different than the spiritual nature of unfallen ones? The quick answer is sin. But let us examine this in context of the Holy Spirit's relationship with angels. The holy nature of the Spirit imparted in an angel is what makes that angel's *spiritual* nature holy. This means that, like us, the only way an angel can be holy is if the Holy Spirit lives in them. Therefore, a fallen angel is unclean because the Holy Spirit does not live in him to cause him to be holy.

This same assumption can be made for the title "Spirit of truth" which tells us that truth can only come from the Holy Spirit—that, and since Christ said "Satan . . . abode not in the truth because there is **no** truth **in** him." Christ is saying that the Holy Spirit, who is truth, does not live **in** Satan. This is important. When the fallen angels were cast out of heaven, their natures became unclean immediately. As soon as they set their hearts to start the war in heaven, the Holy Spirit withdrew Himself from living in them. Thus, they were cast out of heaven and to the earth as unfilled angels. Sin replaced the Holy Spirit's presence in them, causing them to become unclean. This is why they are called unclean angels, because sin and not the Holy Spirit lives in them now.

The Holy Spirit's relationship with fallen angels is different from His relationship with holy angels. Holy angels are filled with the Spirit, move in the Spirit, and do the works of the Spirit. In contrast, the Holy Spirit does not function in and through fallen angels. Rather,

He keeps them alive. Having a life kept alive by the Holy Spirit is the only spiritual privilege fallen angels receive now.

In addition to this, the only reason they are alive is because Christ's life causes *all things to have life*. But God, knowing the power of His life to keep all things alive, disallowed Himself from living in anything unclean. Why? To prevent the eternal nature of His life from keeping a sinful life alive eternally. Therefore, since the eternal nature of God's life does not live in fallen angels, they consequently have a temporary life. Their lives are temporarily kept alive to preserve them until the day the Godhead will destroy them.

Are you now able to see that the only privilege the fallen angels have is that the Holy Spirit is keeping them alive? Family, the fallen angels are on death row! They will walk their last mile. They will bow one last time. They will take their last breath. And when they die, they will never know they lived. They will never know God created them. It will be as if they never existed. Poof. They're gone! Forever! This is God's wrath made perfect in the face of spiritual treason, upheaval, and blasphemy.

My appeal to you is this. If the Holy Spirit daily sustains the life of a fallen angel who sins and wars against Him continuously with sinfulness more hideous than we can imagine, know that the Holy Spirit is always ready to do more for you, whose life is nowhere as terrible as a fallen angel's life. Again, if the Spirit willingly sustains the lives of devils whom He, the Father, and Son will cast into the fire, He will do much more for you, whom He wills to take to glory. Stir up your faith to believe the Holy Spirit wants to do more for you. Your life is more precious to Him than the fallen angels' lives. Jesus died to save *you*, not them! The Holy Spirit came to convert *you*, not them! And the Father wrote *your* name in the book of life, not theirs! Let the Holy Spirit reign in you, friend.

SECOND REVELATION—MATTHEW 25:41

The second revelation, from Matthew 25:41, reads, "Everlasting fire, prepared for the devil and his angels."

Oh, great day! Oh, great day! This text is among one of the most liberating texts! When Adam and Eve sinned, Jesus became the Godhead's solution for humanity's sin problem. But when the fallen angels sinned, the Godhead's solution for their sin was to create hell. The above text says that the "everlasting fire [hell] **was prepared for** the devil and his angels."

Friend, rejoice. God never created hell for us. He created it for the fallen angels. God never intended for us to go to hell, only the fallen angels. Hell came into existence as a solution for their sin, not ours. Christ is the solution to our sins. The Godhead, from the beginning, before Adam and Eve were created, created hell as an eternal solution for the sins the fallen angels committed against them. And again, the Godhead, before Eve ate the fruit, sanctified Christ's blood as a get-out-of-hell-free card for every believer who repents. Therefore, to every human repeat offender, hear this: Jesus is our get-out-of-hell-free card.

But to every fallen angel, hear this: woe unto you! For the dread of God's glory is upon you to destroy you and to bring you to ashes upon the earth. Christ's blood is laid to your charge and is on your hands. You have trespassed against the Holy Ghost to war against His omnipotence and legitimacy to every human life. You have violated heaven and committed spiritual treason in an attempt to take the Father's throne, and you have made the earth desolate and reeking of sin! Woe unto you, fallen angels. Woe unto you, and prepare yourself for the day of Christ's vengeance! To whom will you cry out for help? And who will come to your rescue?

THIRD REVELATION—HIS CHURCH, CHRIST'S CHURCH

The following table will display texts about Satan's church next to texts that speak about Christ's church. Before reading the paragraph that follows the table, notice the similarities and the differences between both churches. May the Holy Spirit enlighten you and increase your understanding. Alleluia, family!

Now get to readin'...hahaha! ☺

The Great Deception	
Satan's Church	**Christ's Church**
Revelation 17:1, 4–5	Revelation 12:1–2, 5
[1]And there came one of the seven angels . . . saying unto me . . . I will show unto thee the judgment of the great whore [Roman Catholic Church] that sitteth upon many waters [people, nations, and tongues].	[1]And there appeared a great wonder in heaven; a woman [Christ's church] clothed with the sun, and the moon under her feet, and upon her head a crown of twelve stars [Twelve Apostles]:
[4] And the woman [Roman Catholic Church] was arrayed in purple and scarlet colour, and decked with gold and precious stones and pearls, having a golden cup in her hand full of abominations and filthiness of her fornication:	[2] And she [Christ's church] being with child cried, travailing in birth, and pained to be delivered.
[5] And upon her forehead was a name written, MYSTERY, BABYLON THE GREAT, THE MOTHER OF HARLOTS AND ABOMINATIONS OF THE EARTH.	[5] And she brought forth a man child [Christ], who was to rule all nations with a rod of iron: and her child [Christ] was caught up unto God, and to his throne [Christ's ascension to glory after His resurrection and after the day of Pentecost].

Boy, is this good. Are you able to see the similarities and differences? If not, the Holy Spirit will walk us through this. Revelation 12 and 17 each talk about a church. Remember, according to Bible prophecy the word *woman* means "church." Specifically, Revelation 12:1–6 is about the New Testament-era church, the church Christ gave rise to when He began His public ministry. His church is made up of the "called out" people of Judaism, idolatry, and paganism, the religions of the first century. Thus, whenever Christ said, "Follow me," He called the Jews out of Judaism and the gentiles out of idolatry and paganism to follow Him. This is how Christ began to build His New Testament-era church, up to our present day and to generations to come. This New Testament-era church is made up of Jews and gentiles and is now governed by the Holy Spirit's law.

Whoa! Ain't God good?

Revelation 17:1–6 is about Satan's work from Babylon to our present day, which gave birth to the Catholic Church in the fourth century. Therefore, in Revelation 17:1, Satan's Catholic Church is described as a harlot to signify that this church is unclean and is not the true church. In Revelation 17:4, the Catholic Church has a lavish description. Words like *precious stones*, *gold*, and *pearls* denote that the wealth of the earth has made her rich. In Revelation 12:1, Christ's church is portrayed as less glamorous. Words like *sun*, *moon*, and *stars* symbolize that the source of the church's power is not from the earth but from the Creator—the one who made the sun, moon, and stars. So far, the difference in the two churches is that Satan's church is adorned with the earth and Christ's church is adorned with the Father's power.

The similarity is they are both churches. But a keen, discerning spirit will notice how Satan's church is a religious organization only and Christ's church is a spiritual body. Satan's church is limited to working through the flesh and sin, while Christ's church operates in the Spirit and through the born-again spirit in man. Can you see the subtle difference between a church that operates as an organized body versus a church led by the Holy Spirit?

Next part.

Satan's Church	Christ's Church
Revelation 17:3	Revelation 12:3–4
And I saw a woman [Roman Catholic Church] sit upon a scarlet coloured beast [papacy], full of names of blasphemy, having seven heads and ten horns [the kingdoms that gave rise to the papacy].	And behold a great red dragon [Satan], having seven heads and ten horns, and seven crowns upon his heads, . . . and the dragon [Satan] stood before the woman [Christ's church] which was ready to be delivered, for to devour her child [Christ] as soon as it was born.

The dragon [Satan] of Revelation 12:3 is in possession and control of the seven heads and ten horns, which in turn, amounts to being in control of the papacy and the Roman Catholic Church. In addition to this, the text, "Satan stood before the woman [Christ's church] . . . to devour her child [Jesus]" is full of significance. First, the words "Satan stood before the woman" literally means that Satan was waiting for God to incarnate Himself as a man. He was plotting against Christ's human life by generationally weakening our human nature with sin. Satan wanted God to be incarnated in the weakest sinful human nature possible.

Second, the words, "Satan stood . . . to devour" reveal how Satan personally wanted to kill Christ. Satan did not assign this task to one of his fallen angels. No, he, without reservation for the consequence of his actions, desired with great hatred to do this evil deed himself. But let us take a moment to understand this from a bigger view of what's going on.

Satan knows who God the Father and God the Holy Spirit are. Before he was cast out of heaven, he stood in their presence as their covering cherub. He, therefore, knew Christ as God and was completely surrendered to His omnipotence. Satan's action to personally kill Christ literally means he wanted to kill God. When the Scripture says, "He stood before the woman to devour her child," know that Satan planned for this day. He waited two thousand years for this day. And he anticipated this moment with the intent to kill God incarnate.

As we move forward, this last table will illustrate Satan's counterfeit church model, contrasting it with Christ's church model.

The Great Deception	
Satan's Counterfeit Church Model	Christ's Original Church Model
Seven Heads and Ten Horns (Babylon, Medo-Persia, Greece, Rome)	Twelve Stars (Twelve Apostles)
Woman—Fourth-century church Catholic Church (Merger of paganism and Christianity)	Woman—First-century church Christ's church (Separation from the old covenant)
Beast—Papacy (Satan's Child)	Child—Christ (The Father's Son)
Dragon—Satan (Built his own church)	Holy Spirit (Holy Spirit builds Christ's church)
Law of Satan's kingdom: Unclean spiritual law, centered on hatred	Law of Christ's kingdom: Holy Spirit's law, centered on love

Satan's great deception is the use of a counterfeit church model to mislead people and to orchestrate his final deception on humanity, which is to merge the secular with religion to form a sinfully profane religious organization.

Saints, do not miss out on heaven. Christ says, "I go and prepare a place for you . . . that where I am, there ye may be also" (John 14:3). Look up! It's almost time to go home. I'll meet you there.

Love,

~Lynet

#glorybound

ABOUT THE AUTHOR

As a worker of the gospel, Lynet Winfrey has touched many through teaching them how to live by Christ's faith and how living by the Spirit's law is essential to their eternal destiny with the Father. Although she is a spiritually profound speaker and writer, she is, at best, a teacher gifted with the ability to communicate the Father's word in a way that the hearer's heart desire will be to draw closer and closer to Him.

Lynet Winfrey Books

Kept by the Word: Unveiling God's Purpose of Prayer

When the Father instituted prayer, He righteously designed it to be equipped with His purpose to accomplish His will. Satan, knowing this, has tried to redefine prayer to have us think that prayer is based on our purpose—not God's. This has led to a misunderstanding and misuse of prayer. In *Kept by the Word: Unveiling God's Purpose of Prayer*, author Lynet Winfrey will give you a faith-filled knowledge of prayer that will cause you to righteously desire to pray the way the Father designed.

Kept by the Word: Spiritual Meat for the Hungry

Kept by the Word: Spiritual Meat for the Hungry was written to help readers enter a deeper spiritual relationship with Christ. Paul in Galatians 2:20 informs how he lives by Christ's faith. What does it mean to live by Christ's faith? Is Christ's faith different from ours?

Hebrews 8:13 expresses how the old covenant vanished away, and Hebrews 8:7 says that a new covenant replaced it. What is the name of both covenants? And how will knowing them impact my life?

Jude 1:6 says that the fallen angels did not "keep" their place in heaven but left. Is there any spiritual insight we can learn from those words when we group them with other scriptural text?

These questions and more will be answered as the book spiritually equips and empowers its reader.

ENDNOTES

1 A.C. Flick, *The Rise of the Mediaeval Church* (New York: Burt Franklin, 1900), 150.

2 Carl Conrad Eckhardt, *The Papacy and World-Affairs* (Eugene, OR: Wipf & Stock, 1937), 1.

3 *Code of Justinian* (*Codex Justinianus*), 1:1.

Made in the USA
Middletown, DE
31 July 2023